The Landlord's Primer
For Georgia

a self help guide for inexperienced landlords

By: Mary Farmer

Published By
GLOBAL INTERESTS PRESS
690 Greystone Park • Atlanta, GA 30324
Phone: 404 892-0100   Fax: 404 872-4591

Copyright © 1993 by Mary Farmer

Cover Design by JEANINE ERCEG
Design and composition by TWIN STUDIOS, *Atlanta, GA*

The Landlord's Primer
For Georgia

ISBN 0-9636735-0-5

Dedication
This book is dedicated to Donna Smith.
Without her encouragement it would not have been written.

Acknowledgements
There are many people I would like to thank for their help and support in preparing this manuscript. First, Michael Dowling, my dear, dear husband; thanks honey. For guidance through the legal maze: Betty Green Berman, Kay Young and the law library staff at Emory University and Georgia State University. For real estate know how: Robert (Bob) Brown, Verlee Fowler, Jane Fullwood and David Rubinger.

Author's Disclaimer
This publication is designed to provide accurate and authoritative information in regard to the subject matter covered. It is sold with the understanding that neither the publisher nor the author is engaged in rendering legal or accounting services. The publisher and author shall not be responsible for any damages resulting from inaccuracy or omission contained in this publication. If legal advice or other expert assistance is required, the services of a competent professional should be sought.

CONTENTS

Chapter One
1 Selecting Good Tenants

Chapter Two
11 The Lease Agreement

Chapter Three
31 Deposits, Administrative and Move In Fees

Chapter Four
37 The Move Out

Chapter Five
43 How To Legally Evict Your Tenant

Chapter Six
65 Other Remedies

Chapter Seven
73 Service Agencies for Landlords

79 Index

Appendix
84 Forms

PREFACE

PLEASE PAY THE RENT ON TIME ... Please return my phone calls ... Please stop your dog from chewing up the doors and carpeting. As letters flew back and forth and my tenant failed to respond, I began to look for answers. Did I have to keep tolerating rude and irresponsible behavior? What recourse did I have? I was angry and outraged over the destruction of my property and frustrated by my lack of knowledge. Does any of this sound familiar? If your answer is yes, read on.

Had I known the basic landlord-tenant laws of Georgia, I could have avoided many unpleasant conversations and nerve-wracking moments. I am not a lawyer and therefore was completely baffled by the legal procedures required of me to conform with the landlord-tenant laws of Georgia. In addition, I could not find anyone who would answer my questions. Some simple, straight answers would have been nice. I just wanted to know what the proper notice period was for terminating a lease.

I did try to sort things out by going to the library and reading the Georgia Code; no luck there. I began to look for other sources of information to assist me and found none. I was truly stuck. My only recourse was to call a lawyer. But which lawyer?

Finding an attorney with specific landlord-tenant experience was quite difficult. When I finally located someone who specialized in landlord-tenant law, I was beside myself. Seeking the advice of a seasoned attorney really opened my eyes. Later, my visits to courtrooms, where dispossessory (eviction) cases are heard, confirmed my suspicions regarding the tremendous need for a landlord's self help guide.

To give you an idea of the magnitude of the problem, 5,000 to 6,000 dispossessory cases are filed each month in Fulton County, Georgia! Yes, 5,000 to 6,000 each month in Fulton County. If there is comfort in numbers, we landlords are a very comfortable group.

I have attempted to give Georgia landlords good, solid information. *The Landlord's Primer* is a beginner's source book. You will be able to sort through many tough questions and be apprised, through this text, of situations you may not have anticipated. Of course, there are nuances and exceptions to every situation. I apologize that I cannot anticipate all of them. It is my sincere hope that I have provided most of the information that you need to successfully manage your rental property but please be aware that laws do change and are subject to differing interpretations. I have tried to insure the accuracy of the information contained herein but remember, I am not a lawyer. My intention is to assist novice landlords, with questions and frustrations like my own, through the system. Once you know the wherefores and how tos, it's not so bad.

Owning and managing rental property is a very honorable business. Current statistics indicate that 52,000,000 people in the United States are renters. If it weren't for us where would all of these folks live? You do not have to take any grief from some tenant who won't pay the rent. Without you s/he'd be on the street and there are plenty of good, responsible renters out there.

Please read this book completely before you put your "for rent" sign out. It addresses only the laws that govern the rental of residential property. I have not provided information for commercial leasing. Furthermore, I have not delved into the realm of Section Eight housing which is government subsidized and governed by federal and HUD guidelines. You will need to contact the housing authority in your county to find this information.

Each county has its own rules, regulations and codes which address fire codes, building codes, sanitation needs and the like. You will want to contact the housing authority in your county for a copy of this information.

In all examples throughout the book I have used the fictitious name of Acme Apartments. I have named my renter Tammy Tenant and I have set her rental amount at $750.00 per month. Tammy Tenant's late fee is $75.00 and Margaret Manager is the landlord. Substitute the name of your own apartment complex or unit, the name of your tenant and the amount of rent you charge each month in each case.

A suggested format for letters, forms and legal notices has also been included. All forms that are provided in the appendix have been set in bold face type on first reference to indicate this. If you have purchased the book, you may copy them as you wish for your personal use. I have given the bare bones information needed. Adjust each form to fit your needs.

Unfamiliar terms have been italicized on first reference and then defined in the text.

I think it's very important that you read through this book one time before you jump into action since most of the information follows a set course. It will not do you any good to look up the dispossessory filing process if you have not completed the strict compliance and demand for possession procedures. If you are confused, that's my point. Read the complete text, even the parts that you are not interested in, before you take any step.

Good luck. I would appreciate any suggestions or comments for improvement in any subsequent editions of *The Landlord's Primer*. Please send all comments or inquiries to the publisher.

CHAPTER ONE

Selecting Good Tenants

Golden Rule #1
Select Good, Rent Paying Tenants

This is the landlord's golden rule. Repeat it over and over until you have it firmly in your mind. Select good tenants now to avoid problems later. The following steps provide a systematic way to limit your risk of renting to unscrupulous tenants.

Qualify all prospects

If you are fortunate enough to select good tenants you will not have to chase after your tenants or face the legal process later to collect the rent. The whole idea of qualification is to weed out undesirable people before they become your tenants. Trying to make this decision based on intuition or 'gut feelings' is foolhardy. Instead, you must obtain verifiable background information on any prospective tenant to help you determine whether or not s/he will be a good tenant.

The qualification process will take some time and effort on your part, but skimping here will cost you dearly later. Just roll up your shirt sleeves and get to it. If you feel that the pre-qualification process is too much work, I suggest that you go to the Magistrate Court, where dispossessory cases are heard, and observe the proceedings for one day. (Dispossessory is the legal term for eviction in Georgia.) It will open your eyes and convince you that careful screening is a must. If you don't know where dispossessory cases are presented look in the Blue Pages™ of your phone book under Magistrate or State Court and call the Clerk's Office for directions.

To begin the qualifying process, have the prospective tenant fill out a **Rental Application** form. A suggested format is provided in the appendix. If more than one applicant, whether roommates or husband and wife, have each person fill out a rental application. When a prospective renter returns the form, review it to make sure all the blanks have been filled in. Make sure the applicant and co-applicant (roommate or spouse) have signed and dated the application. Do not let the length of this form intimidate you. You will need all of this information to make a valid judgment regarding the tenant worthiness of the person or persons applying for residence in your property.

Do not be satisfied simply because the form is filled out. Carefully scrutinize each line contained in the rental application. If you note any of the following, do not rent your property to this person:

- Applicant does not have a checking account.
- Applicant has had three or more addresses in past two years.
- Applicant is 32 years old, married and states s/he has lived with mother for the last 12 years.
- Applicant has had several jobs or unstable employment in the past two years.
- Applicant failed to inform you of negative notations in his/her credit report.
- You discover some hidden problem.

Make sure you look at the applicant's driver's license and a credit card to verify his or her identity. Intuition is not good enough. If there is *any* discrepancy ask about it. For instance, the driver's license may show an address not indicated on the rental application. This is a possible red flag. Make it your business to know why. After all, you are giving consideration to this person to live in *your* property. Liars and cheats are not welcome.

Preliminary checkpoints

Before going to the trouble of checking out the applicants' income, credit and previous landlords, ask them the following questions:

- WHEN ARE THE TENANTS READY TO OCCUPY YOUR UNIT? If they want the place three months from now there is no need to spend any more time with them. You want someone who can occupy your dwelling as soon as possible. Find out when their current lease expires. Make sure the current landlord verifies the expiration date of the lease.

- DO THEY HAVE ENOUGH MONEY TO COVER THE DEPOSIT AND RENT? You can find out by taking a **Request for Verification of Deposit** form to the applicants' bank and confirming that funds are available to cover the move-in fees. Do not accept a personal check for the first month's rent or move in fees. Take cash, money orders, or cashier's checks only. Ask how much deposit they are prepared to pay. If it is less than you require, there is no need to proceed any further.

- HOW MANY PEOPLE INTEND TO OCCUPY THIS SPACE? While you cannot discriminate on the basis of race, religion, national origin, sex, familial status or handicap, you can limit the number of occupants of your property. A two bedroom apartment simply cannot provide adequate room for six or seven people. Furthermore, the wear and tear will send you to the poorhouse when it comes time to re-rent and you have a lot of repairs to make. Remember, you cannot use this rule selectively. A studio or efficiency may be occupied by one person, a one bedroom may be occupied by two people, and a two bedroom may be occupied by four people. The rule of thumb is two people per bedroom. In addition, you can further specify that children of the opposite sex be housed in different bedrooms. *Check your local fair housing rules to be sure you don't violate any law.*

- DO THEY HAVE PETS? You, Mr./Ms. Landlord, will be best served by sticking to a strict *no pet* policy. I know Fido is cute, but make an exception and you will surely regret it. Many tenants think they can sneak in one tiny kitten. Determine if they are pet owners before they get wind of your no pet policy. For some reason rental property is treated with disdain. Pet accidents and destructive behaviors are tolerated by tenants. A previous tenant of mine allowed her dog to chew and scratch up door facings, dig up electrical wires and destroy shrubbery.

  Prospective tenants often lie about pets and the number of people living with them. You may be able to obtain this information by asking the questions in such a way as to not reveal your feelings.

- DO THEY HAVE A WATERBED? Don't allow waterbeds or other water-filled furniture since potential damage from weight or water is too great for you to risk.

- DO THEY SMOKE? This may be hard to understand, but it is a wise policy. Smokers are a fire hazard. You may not selectively apply this policy. If you enforce a strict and consistent "no smoking" policy you may refuse to rent to an applicant based on this alone.

- WHAT KIND OF VEHICLES DO THEY HAVE? No motorcycles, trucks with ladders and signs, etc. You don't want any loud, oversized or disabled vehicles parked on the premises. It makes a mess and really upsets the neighbors.

Gather as much information about the applicant as you can. If they fail to give you straight, no-nonsense answers to your questions, be very warry. I would not rent to someone who is evasive or vague when answering questions.

Background check

After you have thoroughly and carefully inspected the rental application, you must document the validity of all information contained in it.

You will need to check employment references, bank references, previous landlord references, the dispossessory index[1] and get a credit report. Whew! It sounds like a lot of work and it is but if you develop a systematic approach you will breeze through this process.

When determining the amount you want to charge for the application fee remember that the bank will want $20.00, the credit bureau will want $20.00 to $30.00 and that you will incur administrative and postage fees. This application fee is non-refundable and not considered part of the security deposit. I suggest an application fee of $30.00 to $75.00.

In order to obtain credit, employment and rental histories, you must inform the prospective tenant that you will conduct a survey of his/her background.

You must have his/her written permission to do so. Note that the sample rental application has an authorization included in it. A copy of this authorization with a letter from you requesting verification is adequate for most banks and employers.

Forms that can be used to request this information are found in the appendix. These have been provided as a convenience. If you have more than one unit you will tire of writing the same letters over and over. Standardize your forms and photocopy them instead of composing a new one each time you need information on a tenant. If you use a computer it will be very easy to design forms to fit your needs.

Have the rental applicant sign as many copies as you will need to get all necessary information. Then, fill in the top part and mail them off.

The four qualifying steps:

1. VERIFY INCOME: *Net* pay or take home pay should equal three times the rent. For instance: If you plan to charge $750.00 per month for your property your prospective renter should *bring home* $2250.00 per month. That is $750.00 X 3 = $2250.00. (Note: I will use the example of $750.00 per month throughout this book so the figures will be uniform. Simply substitute your monthly rental fee any time you see $750.00.)

   You can verify the applicant's income with pay stubs from his or her employer or from a credit reporting agency. (See chapter seven for guidelines on selecting an agency.) Again, you must obtain the applicant's permission to investigate his/her credit and employment. While marital status cannot be used as a deciding factor, you may require that each adult occupant have net income equal to three times the rent. If a divorce or break up should occur, you do not want to be stuck with the spouse who has no income.

   Have the prospective tenant sign the authorization line on the Request for Verification of Deposit and **Employment Verification** forms. (See appendix.) The combined information will allow you to determine if the applicant meets your minimum income requirement. You will want to make sure that bank balances correlate to payroll deposits. Large monthly withdrawals that leave low daily balances may indicate some problem.

   You have a right to know this information. Do not feel like you are invading the privacy of Mr. or Ms. Tenant. You will be glad that you took the time to be thorough in your selection process. If the tenant stops paying rent, your payments—mortgage, insurance, utilities, taxes, upkeep and maintenance—go on while the tenant enjoys the luxury of your property rent-free. Be well advised that many tenants know the eviction game only too well. They know how long they can stay and what tasks *you* have to perform before they can be legally ejected from your rental unit.

   Set high standards and stick to them. Do not compromise when it comes to tenant selection.

2. **VERIFY INCOME STABILITY:** Using the written permission you have secured from the prospective tenant, verify his/her employment. If that person has been on the job for less than six months do not rent to him/her. Chances are this person not only goes from job to job but s/he also goes from house to house leaving a string of unpaid rents in his/her wake.

   Make sure the applicant signs separate forms for current job, previous job and the spouse/co-applicant's current job. You will need three different employment verification forms, which are located in the appendix.

   I know you want to help out that nice person but please don't be tempted to abandon your careful selection process. **In the rental business, no good deed goes unpunished.** If you want to do charity work, volunteer your services at a homeless shelter, domestic abuse shelter or a local AIDS organization. Do not do charity work by providing free housing.

3. **CHECK CREDIT:** Investigate the credit reporting services in your area before you choose one. Explain that you are a property manager and will need credit information on prospective tenants. Interview several agencies and determine which one best suits your needs. (See chapter seven for more information on credit reporting agencies.) If you discover *any* negatives, pass. Be very skeptical of someone who does not tell you that there is some negative history on his/her credit report. If there has been any misunderstanding or inaccurate reporting the prospective tenant should tell you immediately. Listen carefully. It's worth discussing with the credit reporting agency too.

   This credit check should also include an asset check. If things don't work out and you end up with a judgment (a court ruling in your favor) against this tenant you want to be sure that s/he has enough assets to pay you. A good rule is five times the rent. Assets can include equity in an automobile or boat, a savings account or an account with a brokerage house.

4. **CHECK PREVIOUS LANDLORDS:** Do not rent to anyone who moves every six months. Something is wrong. The previous landlord is obligated to honestly answer the following questions:
   - What are the dates the tenant leased/rented?
   - What is the payment history, including late payments?
   - How much is/was the rent?
   - Would landlord re-rent to this tenant? (This question is vital. Make sure the previous landlord gives you an honest answer.)
   - Were there any complaints from neighbors? Any letters to that effect on file?
   - Is the tenant clean? Did s/he leave the unit clean?
   - Why is the tenant moving? Did s/he give proper notice?
   - Was any damage done to the rental unit by this tenant?

Make sure you ask the previous landlord(s) each of the above questions. If the applicant was ever late or habitually late do not rent to this applicant. Obtaining timely rental payment is crucial to being a successful landlord.

If a previous landlord would not re-rent to the person attempting to rent your property then forget it. This is an automatic "do not rent to me" red flag.

Make sure the tenant's reason for leaving his/her current address is the same reason the landlord gives.

Make sure you are talking to a legitimate landlord. A common trick for applicants is to give the name of a relative or close friend as the previous landlord. Of course, this "landlord" will give a positive report on your applicant. When calling an individual, do not divulge that you are a landlord until you are certain who is responding to your reference check.

The appendix contains a worksheet for your use when calling previous landlords. Documentation is important in case you reject an applicant and the rejected party claims some sort of discrimination. If you rejected a prospective tenant because they were habitually late paying their rent to a prior landlord, say so. Document it on the application and file it for three years.

Let me review the qualifying process so far. When the prospective renter fills out the application, make these preliminary checks:
- Ask for move in date.
- Verify that sufficient funds are available for move in fees.
- Ask how many occupants.
- Verify no pets.
- Verify no waterbeds.
- Verify no smoking.
- Check number/type of vehicles.

Next, go through the four qualifying steps:
- Verify income/employment.
- Check income stability.
- Check credit.
- Check with previous landlord.

Having made it through the initial qualifying steps, let's move on to the final round. I know this is tedious. Please console yourself by realizing that this process is designed to protect you, your investment and your sanity.

Final round of the qualifying process

1. PERSONAL REFERENCES. Require at least one local reference. You may ask the reference to refer you to someone else who knows your prospective tenant since you can count on the reference to give a glowing report. Think about the times you have been personally called upon as a reference. Did you make negative comments about your friend or colleague?

   Try to seek other sources. "Thank you Ms. Smith. Can you suggest the name of someone else who could give Ms. Prospective Tenant a recommendation?"

   Collection agencies suggest that you verify family information. It is a fairly common practice for someone to get an apartment, realize they cannot afford it and return to the family home. Knowing where to find someone's mother, father, aunt or uncle can be helpful when trying to track down a renter who has skipped out or abandoned the property.

2. INTELLIGENCE AND ATTITUDE. These qualities are very subjective and very important. You want a tenant of average or above average intelligence. Your conversation while you go over forms and rules will be the most effective way for you to determine this.

   Do not rent to people with negative attitudes. These people will have no regard for paying their rent or treating their rental unit with pride. If you encounter anyone who feels that they are owed something, watch out!!

   I recently saw a van with lemons and negative slogans painted all over it. Can you imagine the extremes this person would go to? I would not rent to any person who appeared on my property in a van with lemons painted on it.

   Try to ascertain whether or not this person drinks excessively or uses illegal substances. It's my experience that all serious addicts know how to lie about their consumption so you may not be able to figure this out. If the prospective tenant presents himself/herself for scrutiny while intoxicated or high, I recommend that you refuse to rent to that applicant.

   I interviewed several eviction service companies and most of them agree that sixty to seventy percent of all evictions are due to the tenant's drug use. The rent money is spent on drugs.

3. CLEANLINESS. The best way to determine this is to visit the prospective tenants in their current dwelling. After you have gone through the qualifying steps, make an appointment to meet the prospective tenants at their house to go over your rental agreement and rules. If they refuse, be very suspicious. Insist that this meeting be held at their current address.

   This is not a decorating call. You want to make sure these people are clean and have pride in their home. Look for glaring red flags like holes in the walls, cigarette burns on furniture and carpets, a month's worth of dirty dishes, drug paraphernalia on the coffee table, etc. You may notice their cat slinking around or worse, the draperies may be in shreds from cat climbing.

Driving by to check things out will be of little benefit if you cannot get inside to note the condition of the current residence.

An important note about discrimination: You may not discriminate or refuse to rent on the basis of race, religion, national origin, sex, familial status (i.e. families with children) or handicap. In addition, if you refuse to permit reasonable modifications, at a handicapped person's expense, to allow his/her full enjoyment of the leased premises you can be charged with discrimination.

Should you not rent to someone because of the information given in the rental application write on the back of the form why you decided against this prospective tenant and keep this record for three years. You never know when someone might file a discrimination suit. You will be able to adequately defend yourself if you apply your rules to all applicants and document why you refused them tenancy.

Make sure you have carefully gone through these steps before the lease/rental agreement is signed. Stress your firm stand on abiding by the rules and paying rent on time. In Georgia, there is no cooling off period. Once the lease is signed it is binding.

---

[1] The dispossessory index is a record of dispossessory cases. It is located in the Clerk's Office of the court house in your county.

CHAPTER TWO

The Lease Agreement

This document is vital to your survival in the landlord vs. tenant world. A lease will provide the basis of your agreement with your tenants and set the guidelines which both you and the tenant must comply with. Make sure the paragraphs included in your lease are ones you can live with.

The lease is written in time-honored legal language. I have included an explanation of each paragraph in layman's terms following the lease. This will give you an understanding of what each paragraph addresses and what choices you have. Read through both the lease and its explanation at least one time before you draft your own lease.

I have tried to anticipate the most likely situations you could face when writing a lease agreement. You do not have to use all that I have written. Pick and choose with care. This lease was constructed to give the landlord as much protection as the law provides.

As of the publication date, these terms complied with Georgia law (Official Code of Georgia Annotated, Title 44 and Georgia Code Annotated, Title 61) as it relates to tenants and landlords for *residential* property only. Do not attempt to use this lease agreement for commercial or Section Eight property. Section Eight pertains to government subsidized rental payments and is administered under different guidelines.

In order to qualify your property for a Section Eight subsidy, federal and HUD guidelines must be complied with. Contact you local housing authority for more information on Section Eight housing.

Things change. I am amazed by the volume of legislation introduced each year to further regulate the residential rental industry. If you have any questions or feel that any section is outdated, check with another property owner, your local apartment owners' association or your lawyer. If you do not know a lawyer call large apartment complexes and ask the name of their tenant/landlord lawyer.

Once again, this is a *residential* rental agreement. Commercial rentals have different rules. Section 8 approved housing is governed by federal law and HUD Guidelines, which supersede Georgia tenant/landlord laws. Residential agreements do not cover the necessary territory for commercial rentals. **Do not** apply one to the other and **do not** attempt to use this guide for anything other than residential property.

GEORGIA RESIDENTIAL RENTAL AGREEMENT

This agreement made this_____day of _____,19___, is between _____(hereinafter called "Landlord") and_____(hereinafter called "Tenant").

Landlord rents to Tenant and Tenant rents from Landlord, __*write in*__ __*address of rental unit*_____, Georgia (hereinafter called "unit") under the following conditions:

1. TERM: FIXED TERM: The initial term of this lease shall be _____, beginning at 12:00 noon _____, 19____, and ending at 12:00 noon, _____, 19____.

   or MONTH TO MONTH: Tenant agrees to lease unit on a month to month basis beginning at 12:00 noon _____, 19____. This lease shall be automatically renewed for additional periods of one month thereafter until terminated by either party giving _____days written notice prior to the end of the rental month.

2. POSSESSION: If there is a delay in delivery of possession by Landlord, rent shall be abated on a daily basis until possession is granted. If possession is not granted within _____ days after the beginning day of initial term, then Tenant may void this agreement and have a full refund of deposit. Landlord shall not be liable for any loss or damages related to such failure to deliver possession in a timely fashion.

3. RENT: Rent is payable monthly in advance at the rate of __*write in the dollar amount of the monthly rent as you do on your checks*__ dollars ($_____) per month, on the first day of each month during the initial or any extended term of this agreement, at the office of Landlord or such other place as Landlord may designate. Rent must be paid on or before the first day of each month at *write the address where you will accept rent payments* . All rent and other charges under this agreement are payable in cash, cashier's check drawn on a local bank, or U.S. Postal Service money order. As a convenience to Tenant, Landlord will accept Tenant's personal check, drawn on a local bank for rent and other payments. In the event that Tenant's check is ever returned for insufficient funds or is not honored for any other reason, Landlord will have the right to require that the returned payment and all future payments be made in cash, cashier's check or U.S. Postal Service money order. If mailed, the rent and all other sums due shall be mailed in sufficient time and with correct postage to be received by Landlord on or before the first day of the month. Landlord is under no obligation to accept personal checks drawn on the account of anyone other than Tenant.

4. LATE CHARGES & RETURNED CHECKS: Under this agreement, rent is due on or before the first day of each month. If Landlord agrees to accept rent after the first day of the month, a late charge of $_____will be due as

THE LANDLORD'S PRIMER

additional rent. In the event any check given by Tenant to Landlord is returned unpaid by the bank, Tenant will be required to pay an additional handling fee of $_____.

5. SECURITY DEPOSIT: Tenant agrees to deposit $_____ with Landlord before taking possession of the unit as security for Tenant's fulfillment of the conditions of this agreement. Security Deposit will be returned to Tenant within thirty (30) days after unit is vacated by all occupants if: lease term has expired or agreement has been terminated by both parties; and all monies due Landlord by Tenant have been paid; and unit is not damaged and is left in its original condition, normal wear and tear excepted. Deposit may be applied by Landlord to satisfy all or part of Tenant's obligations, including but not limited to: any failure to comply with move out procedures, damage not considered wear and tear, damages due to negligence, carelessness, accident or abuse, any unpaid sums due Landlord under the terms of this lease including: rent, late charges, returned or dishonored checks, pet damage, key replacement, charges for removing, packing and storing abandoned seized or lawfully removed property, court costs and any actual damages caused by any breach of this lease by Tenant and such act shall not prevent Landlord from claiming damages in excess of the deposit. Tenant agrees not to apply the deposit to any rent payment, and also agrees to pay $_____ for re-keying locks if all keys are not returned.
(Select A or B below.)
A) Tenant's security deposit is protected by a surety bond on file with the Clerk of Superior Court in the County in which the unit is located or
B) Tenant's security deposit will be deposited by landlord in Escrow Account Number _____ at _name of bank or other financial institution_.

Tenant acknowledges that s/he has been given a list of any existing damages to unit, given the right to inspect the unit and has approved said list except as specified in writing to Landlord. In the event of a sale or other conveyance of the property, Landlord shall be entitled to transfer the security deposit to the party who acquires the property and from and after such transfer Landlord shall be released of any liability with respect thereto.
Any security deposit refund shall be paid to _name of one person who has signed the lease_.

6. NON REFUNDABLE CLEANING FEE: Tenant has deposited with landlord the sum of $_____, as a non-refundable cleaning fee.

7. DISCLOSURE: _you, property manager, landlord, etc._ whose address is_____, is authorized to act on behalf of Landlord with respect to this agreement, to manage the premises, and is owner's duly designated agent for service of process with respect to any matter arising under this agreement. _Person named above_ is authorized

THE LEASE AGREEMENT

to receive notices and demands which relate to this rental agreement on behalf of landlord.

8. EXTENDED/RENEWAL TERMS: Either party may terminate this agreement by giving the other party thirty (30) days written notice prior to the end of the initial term, but if no such notice is given by either party, then this agreement will be automatically extended on a month to month basis (or any time limit you choose) with all terms remaining the same until terminated by either party upon thirty (30) days written notice. Landlord may increase the monthly rent during any extended term by giving Tenant written notice at least thirty (30) days before the date on which such monthly increase shall take effect. *(This does not apply to month to month leases).*

or AUTOMATIC EXTENSION: Landlord or tenant shall notify the other that automatic extension is not desired. Such notice shall be written and delivered thirty (30) days prior to the expiration date of the term of the lease. If no such written notice is received this lease will automatically be extended for one year (six months, ninety days). The same terms and conditions of this lease, except that rent for each such extension period shall be increased by ten percent (10%) over the rent for the preceding term.

9. EARLY TERMINATION: Tenant may terminate this agreement before the expiration of the initial term by giving Landlord thirty (30) days written notice; plus paying all monies due through date of termination; plus paying $_____ as a cancellation fee; plus paying a pro-rated portion of expenses for repainting and cleaning based on the number of months remaining in the initial term to the number of months originally in the initial term.

10. NO ASSIGNMENT OR SUBLETTING: Tenant may not sub-let unit or assign this lease.

11. UTILITIES: Tenant agrees to pay all utilities and services with the exception of the following which Landlord agrees to pay: *list all that landlord will provide* . If cost to Landlord of providing any of the listed utilities increases during the term of this agreement, Tenant shall pay, as additional rent, its share of such increase.

12. NUMBER OF OCCUPANTS: The number of occupants is limited to_____. Only the following persons shall occupy this unit:_____
_____*name and social security number*_____ .

13. FIRE AND OTHER CASUALTY: If the unit is made uninhabitable by fire or other casualty, no fault of the Tenant, this agreement shall be terminated. Tenant releases, holds harmless and indemnifies Landlord from and against any and all claims for loss or damages to person or property arising from or related to such fire or other casualty.

14. HOLD OVER: Tenant shall deliver possession of unit in good order and repair to Landlord upon termination or expiration of this rental agreement. If Tenant holds over and fails to move out on or before the termination date of this lease, the rent for the hold over period shall be an amount equal to one hundred and fifty percent (150%) of the rental rate of the last month of the lease term. Nothing herein shall be construed as consent by Landlord to Tenant to hold over.

15. RIGHT OF ACCESS: Upon serving "Intention to Enter" notice Landlord may enter the unit for inspection and maintenance during reasonable hours. In case of emergency, Landlord may enter at any time. Tenant authorizes Landlord to enter the unit, at any reasonable time, to show the unit to prospective renters after Tenant has given notice of termination.

16. USE: Tenant agrees to use unit for residential purposes only and it shall be occupied only by person(s) named in Paragraph 12. Tenant agrees they will not engage in any illegal activities on the premises nor will they allow others to engage in any illegal activities on the premises insofar as they have the power to stop such activities.

17. PROPERTY LOSS: Landlord shall not be liable for damage, theft, vandalism, or other loss of any kind to Tenant's personal property or the personal property of Tenant's family members or guests, except where such damage is due to Landlord's negligence. It is understood and agreed that Landlord shall not be responsible or liable to Tenant or to those claiming by, through or under Tenant for any loss or damage to either person or property that may be occasioned by or through the acts or omissions of persons occupying adjacent, connecting or adjoining premises, or by or through the acts or omissions of third parties. Landlord encourages Tenant to purchase comprehensive property insurance against all perils, including but not limited to insurance on personal property or property of other persons from protection of loss due to or caused by theft, vandalism, bursting or breaking pipes by or from fire, windstorm, hail, flooding, leakage, steam, snow or ice, by or from running water, backing up of drainage pipes, seepage or the overflow of water or sewage on the property of which Tenant's unit is a part. Landlord shall not be responsible or liable for any injury, loss or damage to any person or property of Tenant or other person caused by or resulting from the aforementioned occurrences. Nothing contained herein shall be deemed to be construed to relieve Landlord of liability for any loss or damage directly caused by or arising from the proven acts of negligence or intentional misconduct on the part of Landlord or directly caused by the proven failure of Landlord to fulfill its obligations under this lease.

18. PETS: No pets, birds or animals of any kind shall be permitted in the unit or on the premises, even temporarily. "Pets" does not include animals trained to serve the handicapped, such as seeing-eye or hearing dogs. These animals may be housed on the premises so long as they are in the direct service of

those they were trained to serve. Landlord will require notice in writing of such service animals on the premises.

19. DEFAULT BY TENANT: Any breach or violation of any provision of this agreement by tenant shall give landlord the right to terminate this agreement or to take possession and hold tenant liable for the remainder of the term. If tenant fails to pay any rent; or other charges when due, or if tenant abandons the unit or fails to perform any of its obligations hereunder, or if any factors contained in tenant's rental application are untrue or misleading, then, upon the happening any of said events, tenant shall be in default hereunder and landlord may at its option terminate this agreement by written notice to tenant. Tenant shall surrender possession of the unit to landlord upon the effective date of such termination notice and Tenant shall be liable to Landlord for, and shall indemnify Landlord against, all rent loss and other expenses (for re-renting, refurbishing, cleaning or otherwise making the unit suitable for re-renting) suffered or incurred by Landlord as a result of Tenant's default and the termination of the agreement. Notwithstanding the commencement of a dispossessory proceeding and the issuance and execution of a writ of possession on account of any default by Tenant, Tenant shall remain liable to Landlord for all rent and other charges accrued through the date on which possession is obtained by Landlord and shall continue to be liable for any rental accruing thereafter until the expiration of the term of this lease or the re-rental of the unit, whichever occurs first.

20. FAILURE OF LANDLORD TO ACT: Failure of Landlord to insist upon strict compliance with the terms of this agreement shall not constitute a waiver of any violation.

21. REMEDIES CUMULATIVE: All remedies under this agreement or by law or equity shall be cumulative. In the event that either landlord or tenant brings legal action to enforce the terms hereof or relating to the leased premises, the prevailing party shall be entitled to all costs incurred in connection with such action including reasonable attorney's fees.

22. NOTICES: Any notice required by this agreement or demand shall be in writing and shall be deemed to be given if delivered personally or by U.S. Mail, certified or registered. From landlord to tenant: notice or demand shall be delivered to the unit cited in this lease agreement or the last known address of tenant, from tenant to landlord: notice or demand shall be delivered to the location where rent is paid,_____*street address*_____, Atlanta, Georgia, _____*zip code*_____.

23. REPAIRS, ALTERATIONS AND DECORATIONS: Tenant accepts unit in the condition as noted on the Security Deposit Inspection form. Landlord will make necessary repairs to unit with reasonable promptness after receipt of written notice from tenant. If any damage, beyond normal wear and tear,

is caused by tenant or his/her guest, tenant agrees to pay landlord the cost of repair with the next rent payment. Tenant may not paint, wallpaper, drill holes, remodel or structurally change unit, nor remove any fixture or appliance therefrom without prior written consent of landlord. Tenant is required to keep unit in a clean, sightly and sanitary condition. Tenant agrees to notify Landlord immediately upon discovering any signs of serious building problems such as cracks in the foundation, tilting porch, crack in plaster or stucco, moisture in the ceiling, buckling sheetrock or siding, leaky roof, spongy floor, leaky water heater or termite activity.

24. ABANDONMENT: If tenant removes or attempts to remove property from the premises other than in the usual course of continuing occupancy, without having first paid landlord all monies due, unit may be considered abandoned, and Landlord shall have the right, without notice, to store or dispose of any property left on the premises by Tenant. Landlord shall also have the right to store or dispose of any of tenant's property remaining on the premises after the termination of this agreement. Any such property shall be considered landlord's property and title thereto shall vest in landlord. Landlord shall have the right to re-rent unit after tenant abandons same.

25. MORTGAGEE'S RIGHTS: Tenant's rights under this lease shall at all times be automatically junior and subject to any deed to secure debt which is now or shall hereafter be placed on premises on which unit is a part; if requested, tenant shall execute promptly any certificate that landlord may request to specifically implement the subordination of this paragraph.

26. LOCKS AND KEYS: Tenant is prohibited from adding locks to, from changing, or in any way altering locks installed on the doors of unit or mailbox unless written permission is granted by landlord. If written permission is granted tenant must immediately provide landlord with a key. There shall be a charge of $_____ to tenant to replace any lost door or mailbox key.

27. WINDOW COVERINGS: All window coverings installed by tenant must be white or lined in white to present a uniform exterior appearance.

28. ANTENNAS: Radio or television aerials shall not be placed or erected on the roof or exterior of buildings.

29. SMOKE DETECTORS: Tenant acknowledges the presence of a working smoke detector on each level of the premises, agrees to keep all smoke detectors located within the unit in working order and further agrees not to disable said smoke detectors in any way. Tenant is responsible for periodic battery replacement. Tenant agrees to report any malfunction, in writing, to landlord.

30. PARKING: Tenant shall be entitled to park _*write number here*_ automobile, bicycle, small passenger van or small passenger truck on the premises. No boat, trailer, motorcycle, camper, large van or large truck of any type, or inoperable vehicle of any description may be parked or left on the premises without prior

THE LEASE AGREEMENT

written consent of landlord. Any non-operative vehicles may be removed by landlord at the expense of tenant owning same, for storage or public or private sale, at landlord's option, and tenant owning same shall have no right of recourse against landlord therefor. If issued by landlord, vehicles must bear parking sticker at all times.

31. STORAGE: No goods or materials of any kind or description which are combustible or would increase fire risks shall be taken or placed in storage areas. Storage in such areas or facilities shall be used wholly at tenant's risk. Landlord will not be liable for any loss or damage.

32. RECREATION AND SERVICE AREAS: Tenant agrees to abide by all rules and regulations now or hereafter established for use of recreation, parking, service and common facilities or areas provided by landlord, all of which are a part of this agreement. Any such facilities or areas shall be used wholly at tenant's risk.

33. GUESTS: Tenant may house any single guest for a maximum period of 14 days consecutively and shall not exceed a total of six weeks per year. Tenant shall be responsible and liable for the conduct of his/her guest. Acts of guests in violation of this agreement or landlord's rules and regulations may be deemed by landlord to be a breach by tenant and subject to termination of this agreement.

34. DECKS, PATIOS, PORCHES, BREEZEWAYS: Balcony or patio shall be neat and clean at all times. No refrigerators or freezers shall be stored and no rugs, towels, laundry, clothing or other items shall be stored, hung or draped on railing or other portions of the balcony, patio, porch, deck or breezeway. The use of outdoor grills of any type is prohibited on decks, patios, screened porches and breezeways. Tenant may not leave any unattended personal property in, on or about any breezeway, walkway, driveway, grounds or other common areas; and any such items so found by landlord may be removed, stored or otherwise disposed of as landlord deems appropriate.

35. WATERBEDS: Tenant shall not have or keep any waterbed or other water-filled furniture in the unit without written permission of landlord.

36. SIGNS: Tenant shall not display any signs, exterior lights or markings on unit. No awnings or other projections shall be attached to the outside of the building of which unit is a part.

37. LANDSCAPING/OUTSIDE MAINTENANCE: Tenant shall be responsible for the routine care and maintenance of the yard and outside areas as follows: *(list all that apply)* mowing lawn, watering lawn, trees and shrubs, removing weeds, raking leaves, removing snow and ice, sweeping walkways etc.

38. ENTRANCES, HALLWAYS, WALKS AND LAWNS: Entrances, hallways, walks, lawn and other public areas shall not be obstructed or used for any purpose other than ingress and egress.

39. WALLS/STRUCTURE: No nails, screws or adhesive hangers except standard picture hooks, shade brackets and curtain rod brackets may be placed in walls, woodwork or any part of unit.

40. PEST CONTROL: Tenant agrees to provide, at his/her expense, pest control and extermination service on the premises and agrees to keep the premises clean and sanitary to avoid problems with insect infestation. Tenant shall notify landlord immediately of any evidence of termite damage.

41. SAFETY: Tenant shall notify landlord of any burned out exterior or hallway lights, faulty locks or lost keys. Tenant shall report to landlord any suspicious persons, strange vehicles or unusual activities. Prior to entry tenant shall demand credentials from any maintenance personnel.

42. COMPLIANCE WITH CONDOMINIUM INSTRUMENTS: Tenant agrees to comply with all terms conditions and provisions of the Condominium Instrument and the Rules and Regulations. Failure to comply with said instrument shall constitute breach of this agreement. Tenant shall indemnify and hold harmless landlord from and against any damages, direct or indirect, incurred by landlord as a result of tenant's noncompliance with any provision of the condominium instruments, rules and regulations.

43. MOVE OUT PROCEDURE: Tenant shall notify landlord thirty (30) days in writing of his/her intent to vacate on or before the expiration of the lease term. At the expiration of the lease term tenant shall totally vacate the unit and remove all trash and items which are not owned by landlord. Tenant shall deliver unit to landlord in identical or better condition than unit was in upon commencement date of this lease, normal wear and tear excepted. Tenant shall leave the floors, patio, balconies, walls, appliances and fixtures clean and in working condition, pay all utility bills, close all windows, lock all outside doors and return all keys to landlord. Tenant shall submit to landlord his/her forwarding address.

44. LANDLORD'S PERMISSION OR CONSENT: If any provision of this agreement requires the written permission or consent of landlord as a condition to any act of tenant, such written permission or consent may be granted or withheld in the sole discretion of landlord, may contain such conditions as landlord deems appropriate and shall be effective only so long as tenant complies with such conditions. Moreover, any written permission or consent given by landlord to tenant may be modified, revoked, or withdrawn by landlord at any time, at landlord's sole discretion, upon written notice to tenant.

45. GENDER: In all references herein to tenant, the use of the singular number is intended to include the appropriate number as the text of this lease may require.

46. NO ESTATE IN LAND: This agreement only creates the relationship of landlord and tenant between landlord and tenant; tenant has a usufruct only and not an estate for years; and no estate shall pass out of landlord.

47. ENTIRE AGREEMENT: This agreement and any attached addendum constitute the entire agreement between landlord and tenant and no oral statements shall be binding.

48. SEVERABILITY: In the event any section of this agreement shall be held to be invalid all remaining provisions shall remain in full force and effect.

49. HOMESTEAD EXEMPTION: Tenant renounces and waives all rights to claim any benefit or exemption under the Homestead Laws of Georgia.

50. RECORDING: This lease shall not be recorded in any public records.

51. TIME IS OF THE ESSENCE: Time is of the essence of this lease and all covenants contained herein.

52. SPECIAL STIPULATIONS: The following special stipulations shall control in the event of conflict with any of the foregoing: *If none, write "NONE".*

IN WITNESS WHEREOF, the parties hereto have caused these presents to be signed in person or by a person duly authorized the day and year above written.

_____   _____
Landlord   Date   Tenant   Date

                                   _____
                                   Tenant   Date

                                   _____
                                   Tenant   Date

Explanation of lease

An explanation of various paragraphs in the Georgia Residential Rental Agreement may be in order. I will try to clear up some of the legal mumbo jumbo. I know it's a pain but the terminology must be correct in your lease or else you'll have no standing if you should need to take court action to enforce the lease agreement.

1. TERM: Defining the "term" establishes a specific time when the lease agreement begins and ends.

   A yearly lease is designed to give the landlord some sense of how long his/her property will be occupied. Select one of the options: fixed term or month to month. Your property will sustain less wear and tear if you can keep it occupied by the same tenant. Moving furniture in and out of your unit will take its toll on carpets, walls, and doorways.

   You may call yourself owner, landlord, management, lessor, etc. You may call the tenant resident, tenant, lessee, etc.

2. POSSESSION: If you cannot deliver the rental unit to the tenant within seven to twenty days of signing the lease you must give them the opportunity to make other arrangements to find a place to live. You must select a number of days between seven and twenty; do not give a range of seven to twenty days. This needs to be a specific amount of time. It is customary to designate seven days. Delay on your part could be construed as injurious or harmful to the tenant.

3. RENT: This procedure outlines your rental collection policy. Make this clear and stick to it! Talk tough and be tough when it comes to collecting rent. Remember this is *your* money.

   Tenants may mail the payment to you. Make sure you specify the address where you want payment sent. You may require payment in person; if so make sure you have a tamper proof drop box so they can pay after hours. More than one tenant has claimed they were unable to pay because no one was in the office.

   You, the landlord, may go to the unit and collect in person. This has the advantage of giving you first hand information on the tenant and how s/he is treating your property. Of course the disadvantage may be listening to a laundry list of complaints. Remind the tenant that complaints must be directed to you in writing.

   You can elect to accept credit cards. If you choose to do this remember there are bank card fees of two to five percent; you may adjust the rent accordingly. You may want to keep an imprinted credit card slip in the file to use for late payment of rent. The tenant will have to agree to this and you must specify what fees will appear on their credit card.

   You may hire a rent collector. This must be someone you trust to collect funds on your behalf. I consider this the least attractive option unless you are physically unable to collect rent or have a morbid fear of the U.S. Postal Service.

   You also want to specify in what form the payment is to be made, the safest being U.S. Postal Service money order, cashier's check from a local bank and cash. You may accept personal checks if you wish. I would abandon any personal check policy with the first bad check. Also remember that people are aware that you are carrying cash. Do not set yourself up for robbery or worse. Take precautions when collecting rent and carrying cash.

   This sample lease agreement protects the tenant from rent increases except those incurred by increasing utilities. If you do not have a lease agreement that specifies what notice is required for raising the rent, you must give a sixty day notice of any rent increase. You can do this as often as you want so long as you give a sixty day notice. You may provide for rent increases in the lease agreement. Most tenants will balk at this; they usually want to lock in their rent payment for the term of the lease.

There is no limit to the amount the rent can be increased unless you set such a limit in the lease. Be prudent.

4. LATE CHARGES & RETURNED CHECKS: Make all late fees stiff!! An inexpensive late fee, say $10.00 to $20.00 will only encourage your tenant to pay late. I suggest a minimum of $35.00. Ten percent of the monthly rent is a customary fee. You may charge per day if you want to. Be aware that judges are put off by *excessive* late fees.

   I sincerely discourage accepting late rental payments. A "third day" stipulation in the lease agreement takes into account that the first may fall on Saturday, Sunday or a holiday. You must use your own judgment on accepting rent payment after the due date. If the due date does not fall on a banking day you should give the tenant consideration for this and accept payment no later that the very next day that the banks are open. This irks me because the tenant is well aware that rent is due "on or before the first of each month".

   Fees for returned checks should be specified as well; remember you'll pay your bank a charge for the returned check and you have to juggle your books to make do until the monies are deposited into your account. I suggest a bad check fee of $20.00 or 5% of the check's amount, is the current legal limit. Make sure you clearly specify late and returned check fees in your lease.

5. SECURITY DEPOSIT: Georgia law requires that you disclose to the tenant the depository and account number where their security deposit resides or post a Surety Bond in the county where the property is located. This is not optional; you must do this.

   The Security Deposit Inventory check list, a mandatory inspection of the property prior to renting, will save you many headaches when the term of the lease has expired. In chapter three, the details of Georgia's Security Deposit law are discussed.

   By law, you must return any unused security deposit money along with an explanation of funds spent to the tenant within thirty days after termination of the lease or *surrender and acceptance* whichever occurs later. Surrender and acceptance means the tenant voluntarily gives up or surrenders possession of the premises and the landlord accepts possesion with the understanding that the lease is terminated. As the landlord, you are required to inspect the property within three business days after termination of the lease or surrender and acceptance of the property. A comprehensive list of damages must be presented to the tenant and s/he has five business days after vacating the unit to inspect.

   Security deposit funds may be used to cover expenses for physical damages caused by the tenant, tenant's guests or household members as well as unpaid rent, late charges, unpaid utilities or actual damages caused by tenant's breach of rental agreement. You cannot keep money to pay for normal wear and tear.

If you specify in the body of the lease agreement what will result in deductions from the security deposit, this will protect you in the event of a dispute.

If there is a dispute please note that current precedent dictates: When the tenant accepts and cashes the check you have written for the security deposit refund s/he has admitted that the landlord's inspection and estimation of damage was correct.

"Any refund shall be paid to _____" makes your work a little easier. Put the name of *one* person who signs the lease. You do not want to have to track down everyone who may have occupied your unit so specify only one name. This is the person to whom you will send any security deposit refund.

If after "reasonable effort" you cannot locate your former tenant, the security deposit is yours ninety days after the date is was first mailed to the tenant and returned undeliverable. Do not fail to call the numbers on the rental application, their last known employer, etc. Be sure that you have exerted reasonable effort to locate the tenant.

6. **NON-REFUNDABLE CLEANING FEE:** This is an optional charge. It is not considered as a part of security deposit funds. It is in your best interest to collect this fee each time you rent the unit to someone. The appendix contains a **Summary of Move In Fees** notice, which lets the tenant know up front how much money s/he will need to move into the unit. It's a great time saver.

7. **DISCLOSURE:** Georgia law requires that a tenant be provided with a written disclosure of ownership. The tenant must have names and addresses of the owner of the premises or the person authorized to act on behalf of the owner to accept service of legal notices, notices required by the lease agreement and complaints. If these names or addresses change, the landlord must notify the tenant within thirty days in writing. You can use U.S. mail or post the notice of change in management/ownership in a conspicuous place. If you own and manage your property, your name and address will be given here.

8. **EXTENDED/RENEWAL TERMS OR AUTOMATIC EXTENSION:** Believe it or not, you have some choices here. You may decide that you do not want a renewal clause. If so, simply state the terms and be done with it. You must give your tenant thirty days written notice that his/her lease is terminated as of the date specified in the lease agreement. If the lease terminates on September 30, do not send the termination letter until after you have collected August rent. Something about those termination notices limits the tenant's desire to pay the rent. If s/he does not pay the final month's rent you will have to get your money by filing dispossessory proceedings, a civil suit for rent, or distress proceedings or you'll have to just hope that the security deposit is adequate to cover unpaid rent and damage repairs.

Automatic renewal (periodic tenancy) will become a *tenancy at will* unless you specify the procedure and time limit for terminating the lease agreement. A tenant at will is occupying your property *with* your permission but does not have a specified term for this tenancy. Under Georgia law a tenancy at will requires thirty days notice on the part of the tenant and sixty days notice on the part of the landlord to terminate the lease. If s/he won't move you must go through dispossessory proceedings to get that tenant out.

If you have a good tenant and want to keep him/her, a tenancy at will agreement will save you both a great deal of paper work.

This will hopefully avoid something aptly called *tenancy at sufferance*. A tenancy at sufferance means the tenant is unlawfully in possession of the property *without* the landlord's consent. Most tenancies at sufferance occur when the tenant *holds over* — i.e. does not move out when the lease expires. You do not want to indicate in any way that you have given permission to this tenant to remain in your property. If you accept any rent payment, you will create a tenancy at will. If s/he will not move you must, once again, resort to dispossessory proceedings to get him/her legally evicted.

9. EARLY TERMINATION: Any lease/rental agreement must be equitable. If the landlord can terminate, then so can the tenant. The terms can be negotiated. Be aware that your tenant could simply abandon the property and you would have to go to court to get any rent due. Early termination clauses give you some hope for fairness.

Military personnel who receive a permanent change in orders or a temporary change lasting longer that ninety days must be given special consideration. This is more than a patriotic duty. Georgia law requires that you terminate the lease of said military person upon receiving a thirty day written notice and verification of the change of orders. If the soldier is required to move sooner you will have to give him/her that opportunity and terminate the lease as soon as you are notified.

10. NO ASSIGNMENT OR SUBLETTING: If you want to lose control of your property, then let your tenants decide who will occupy it. Can you think of a better way for a tenant to show displeasure? Under no circumstances allow the tenant to assign or sublease your property.

11. UTILITIES: Utilities can be a big bother. If possible let each tenant pay for his/her utilities. If your building has one central meter you will have to prorate the utilities and decide how much you want to charge each tenant each month. Specify clearly which utilities are covered by the rent. For instance: "Cold water only" or "None" or "Gas, electricity, water and trash pick up".

It is amazing how careless people will be when they are not responsible for the monthly power, gas and water bills. Many landlords make sure that heating and air conditioning controls are well out of sight of wasteful tenants. Simply placing them in a locked box is not enough. Make sure the thermostat cannot be seen or manipulated.

A landlord told me that his tenants placed ice cubes on the plexiglas box securing the thermostat so the furnace would run non-stop. He soon installed another thermostat, in a locked utility closet, and let the tenants believe their ice cube trick worked.

12. NUMBER OF OCCUPANTS: One sure way to wear our your property is to allow a passel of folks to live in it. Each person that lives in the unit will contribute to normal (and abnormal) wear and tear. Do not allow more people than dictated by local fair housing rules to occupy your rental property.

13. FIRE AND OTHER CASUALTY: This clause will terminate your obligation to provide housing for the tenant if the unit is uninhabitable because of fire or other major catastrophe. If the fire or casualty is the tenant's fault s/he is still obliged to pay rent for the term of the lease. Of course you have to prove this and most likely will have to sue the tenant to collect the money due.

14. HOLD OVER: A tenant who is holding over is one who has failed to move out of the property when the lease has expired. This paragraph specifies that you have not given your permission for the tenant to stay after the lease has expired. The type of tenancy, tenancy at will or tenancy at sufferance, is important if you have to seek legal action to regain possession of your property. The rent increase is intended to encourage the tenant to move out or sign a new lease. It is a collectable amount. In Georgia, courts have recognized up to double the current rent.

15. RIGHT OF ACCESS: It is inevitable that you will need to get into the unit for some valid reason. It is good tenant/landlord manners to give a written notice before doing so.

    You may state in the lease that you can enter without notice. This paragraph would state: *"Landlord may enter without notice during reasonable hours to perform repairs, routine maintenance or inspect the unit."* This is not a wise policy and may get you into some unforeseen trouble. The tenant could accuse you of theft, damage, rape, trespass or other crimes.

    Of course, in the case of emergency (fire, flood, storm damage, etc.) you are entitled to free access.

    When the tenant notifies you of his/her desire to terminate the lease you will want to show the property so you can get new tenants as soon as possible. Give yourself the "right" to show the unit at any "reasonable" time. You know this means you can't show the apartment at two in the morning. Be as considerate as you can; your prospective tenant will be watching how you treat your current tenant. You don't want to scare off a good prospect because you appeared inconsiderate or pushy.

16. USE: You definitely do not want your tenant operating a business out of your rental unit. This traffic from customers will add to wear and tear. Liability for the tenant's customers, should someone injure themselves on the premises, could fall squarely on your shoulders.

17. PROPERTY LOSS: You should insure the rental unit/building and any related buildings. You are not required to insure the tenant's belongings. This does not release you from liability for any injury caused by your negligence. Make sure your property is safe. A **Hazard** letter is provided in the appendix.

    If your tenant can prove that s/he gave you notice of any defective condition of the premises, s/he can recover damages from you for any injury resulting from defects in the premises. Investigate and act on any report of defect or malfunction in your property. You might want to give your tenant a written report of the repairs done.

18. PETS: I am a pet lover and therefore very aware of the damage they can do. Tenants generally aren't terribly concerned about your property anyway and they will allow their pets to do unspeakable deeds to your carpeting, draperies, walls, door facings, etc. The wise landlord strictly enforces a no pet policy.

19. DEFAULT BY TENANT: This gives you the right to terminate the lease for any breach of its terms. Without this express right you have a lease that you cannot successfully enforce. Make sure your lease clearly states: "ANY BREACH OR VIOLATION." In order to terminate the lease under this provision you must give two separate notices to the tenant. The first notice will specify the breach or default; i.e. "you have operated a business in your rental unit," and give the tenant ten day to cure this breach. If the tenant fails to cure the breach the landlord then sends a letter indicating that the lease has been terminated. The letter must state: "Your lease is terminated" and "Demand for immediate possession is hereby made." If the tenant fails to vacate in twenty four hours you may begin dispossessory proceedings.

20. FAILURE OF LANDLORD TO ACT: In case you missed a breach of the lease agreement, you do not want your oversight to limit your ability to enforce the terms of the lease. The mere act of omission can be construed as permission and you do not want to give your tenant permission to break any of the rules or terms specified by this lease agreement.

21. REMEDIES CUMULATIVE: If you can collect legal fees, so can the tenant. A Georgia court will not recognize your right to collect fees unless the tenant has the same right. You may choose to exclude this whole clause. A responsible landlord will want to include this clause as s/he is reasonably sure that s/he will prevail in a court case. If you have adopted underhanded ways and do not perform as the law requires, including this paragraph could end up costing you a bundle.

    In dispossessory cases court costs (not attorney's fees) are included in the judgment if you ask for them.

22. NOTICES: This sets up the mechanism for sending notices to each other, for example, if the tenant needs to report repairs or you need to notify of intent to enter, demand for possession, etc. First class mail cannot be refused.

23. **REPAIRS, ALTERATIONS AND DECORATIONS.** This provision makes it clear that the tenant is not to engage in any unauthorized decorating. Tenants are notorious for sloppily hanging hideous wallpaper and painting rooms colors akin to worm intestines.

    You also want to prevent your tenant from structurally altering the premises.

    It is the duty of the landlord to keep the premises in repair. You *cannot* avoid or transfer this duty!! The landlord must make repairs and improvements in order to maintain buildings within city/county codes and ordinances. If you should discover a defect that requires repair, written notice is not required because you personally obtained the knowledge. There is no excuse or legal remedy for avoiding these repairs.

    The tenant may have the repairs done and withhold payment for them from the rent if you don't act in "reasonable time" on a request for repair. If the tenant has notified you in writing that repairs need to be made and you have not made the repairs in "reasonable time" (a jury will decide what is "reasonable time") the tenant can make repairs and send receipts for the repairs instead of rent.

    Think about your tenant selecting the workers who will make repairs on your property. I am very uncomfortable with the idea of tenants making decisions like this. You could be charged an outrageous amount because the tenant did not shop the price or be left with inferior work because the tenant selected his/her cousin Joey to make the repairs.

    If your failure to make repairs causes the tenant any property damage or personal injury you can be sued. The tenant must have evidence that proves willful misconduct, malice, fraud, wantonness, oppression, conscious indifference or negligence on your part.

24. **ABANDONMENT:** Exactly how to determine abandonment is not clearly defined in the Georgia Code. You have several options when you discover your property "abandoned". You may terminate the lease, re-rent the dwelling and charge the abandoning tenant any deficiency, sue for breach, institute dispossessory proceedings or permit the premises to remain vacant and seek a judgment for rent due.

    It's clear that your tenant is skipping out when they move their furniture out of the unit at midnight. You will want the ability to clean the unit and re-rent it as soon as possible. Many landlords assume the property abandoned if there is no food in kitchen area and all or most of the clothing has been removed.

    Use prudence when labeling your property abandoned. If you learn that the premises have been vacated (tenant is not using them) and you feel that the tenant's remaining personal property has been abandoned, you, (the landlord), are entitled to enter the dwelling and remove it without benefit of dispossessory action.

I recommend that you photograph all of the personal property and carefully list each item and its condition. You may put the personal property in storage or dispose of it. If you choose the former, write a letter to the tenant at his/her last known address informing them that you have removed and stored their property. Make sure that you have a responsible person, who will be a good witness assist you in disposing of or storing the tenant's abandoned property.

The photos will provide a clear record of what was stored and/or disposed of. You can bet that a tenant has returned to claim that there was $5,000.00 sewn into the sofa cushion. Keep all documentation for future use if the tenant should make such a claim.

The lease must state that any abandoned property shall be considered landlord's property and title thereto shall vest in landlord. This makes clear that any property abandoned by a tenant will become the landlord's to dispose of as s/he wishes.

The safest way to handle abandoned property, if you are not completely certain, is to follow the dispossessory process (see chapter five) and have the court grant possession to you via a *writ of possession*. This document, which is issued by the Clerk's Office in your county, transfers possession of the property back to you, the landlord, and cancels the lease.

25. MORTGAGEES' RIGHTS: This gives the mortgage holder the right to use the property to satisfy any debt against it. If you should default, your banker will want the right to sell the property.

26. LOCK AND KEYS: Changing locks presents many problems: you cannot enter the property, re-keying locks can be very expensive and it puts more bolt holes in your doors.

    Make sure that all pass keys are kept in a secure and safe place. If a tenant should be harmed because an unauthorized person obtained access with your key and the tenant sues, you can be held liable.

27-41. GENERAL RULES AND REGULATIONS: Look around your property. You may have other needs not listed here. I tried to think of as many as possible, but each unit and location present a different set of circumstances. Make sure you cover yours.

42. COMPLIANCE WITH CONDOMINIUM INSTRUMENTS: If your unit is located in a condominium area make sure they will allow you to lease it out. You must require your tenant to abide by all of the condo rules, or the Condo Association will be all over you. You must attach a copy of that document to the lease if it is part of the lease. Have the tenant initial all pages of the copy.

43. MOVE OUT PROCEDURE: This will save you aggravation in the end. If you establish a move out procedure, reinforce it in a letter and give the tenant some general guidelines. It *is* possible to have a happy move out.

44. LANDLORD'S PERMISSION: If you decide to give a tenant permission to install a water bed and the tenant below him/her begins to notice a sag in the ceiling you will want the opportunity to withdraw the okay on that water bed.

45. GENDER: Make sure you don't accidentally exclude anyone.

46. NO ESTATE IN LAND: This is to protect you from the tenant's heirs. Should the tenant die the lease terminates and you do not have to take on his/her "no account" relative as a tenant.

47. ENTIRE AGREEMENT: This means you have clearly stated your terms in their entirety in this lease. There are no secret clauses or other agreements outside of this lease in effect.

48. SEVERABILITY: In the event any part of the lease should be voided or unenforceable you don't want the whole document thrown out. This will allow all but the invalid portion of the lease to stand.

49. HOMESTEAD EXEMPTION: Renters are not entitled to homestead exemption and you do not want anyone else to apply their name to your tax records. This could cause all kinds of problems with title.

50. RECORDING: Any public recording of the lease may cause problems with the landlord's ability to prove clear title on the property. If you are seeking loans or other financing you may not be able to show clear title. This would really make you nuts.

51. TIME IS OF THE ESSENCE: This is supposed to ensure strict compliance. It's here for whatever it may be worth.

52. SPECIAL STIPULATIONS: This is for any type of extraordinary circumstance not covered in your lease.

Each adult authorized to occupy this unit should sign the lease. You want someone to go after in the event of default, non-payment of rent or breach of some lease provision. Make sure you know who is signing this lease. They are the people you will name in the case of a dispossessory or other proceeding.

If the property is furnished list all the furnishing on a separate "schedule A" and attach it to the rental/lease agreement. This list should indicate any previous damage and the current condition of the furnishings so it will be clear what damage resulted from tenant abuse.

CHAPTER THREE

Deposits, Administrative and Move In Fees

Golden Rule #2
Never accept a personal check for deposits, first month's rent or other move in fees. Require this payment by cashier's check, cash or money order.

Georgia Security Deposit Act

The Georgia Security Deposit Act requires that any security deposit funds collected by the landlord be held in escrow or protected by a *surety bond* for the term of the lease. A surety bond is a guarantee that the funds will be available when the lease is terminated. Landlords must inform the tenant of location and account number where security deposit monies have been deposited. The escrow account must be in a bank or lending institution subject to regulation by the State of Georgia or any agency of the United States Government.

Security deposits may be used for repair of damages, unpaid rent, late fees, pet fees, unusual cleaning fees, damages due to abandonment, utility payments, actual damages caused by tenant's breach of lease, repair work or cleaning contracted by the tenant with third parties and others.

You may deposit this money in an interest earning account. To encourage your tenant to follow your move out procedure (covered in chapter six), you may voluntarily pay the interest earned to the tenant or you may keep any interest earned for yourself. I would strongly consider offering it to your tenant. It's no skin off your nose and the simple gesture of offering the tenant interest on his/her security deposit funds may save you some aggravation upon termination of the lease. It is an exercise of good will.

The landlord may post and maintain an effective surety bond with the clerk of the superior court in the county where the dwelling is located. The amount of the bond shall be the total amount of the security deposits which the landlord holds on behalf of the tenants or $50,000.00, whichever is less. The bond is executed by the landlord as principal and a surety company authorized and licensed to do business in the state of Georgia.

As landlord you are responsible for repairs (leaking roof, electrical problems, etc.). These repairs cannot be deducted from the security deposit. Your tenant is responsible for damages which occur after s/he moves in. This does not include normal wear and tear. All damages due to negligence of the tenant, tenant's family, guests or other visitors are the responsibility of the tenant and must be paid directly by the tenant or deducted from the security deposit when the tenant moves out.

Nothing in the lease can eliminate the landlord's duty to perform repairs and exempt him/her from refunding unused security deposit money. Do not try to get around this as you cannot legally remove your responsibility to make necessary repairs.

Security deposit inspection

Georgia law also requires a security deposit inspection. Anyone who owns fewer than ten rental units and manages them him/herself is not required to follow those inspection procedures unless the services of a property manger are utilized. However, as a precaution I recommend that all landlords follow these procedures—which must be carried out by the property manger. Below is the required procedure for the move in as dictated by Georgia law:

> A written list of any existing damages must be given to the tenant prior to the payment of security deposit and prior to moving into the rental unit. Attached to this list must be a notice to the tenant that s/he must acknowledge the correctness of the **Move In Inspection** list by signing it. If s/he does not agree with the information on the form s/he must file a properly signed written statement of dissent setting forth specifically those items with which tenant disagrees.

Photos taken in the presence of the tenant can be helpful too. You may attach them to the inventory to substantiate your claims at the move out inspection.

Please see the appendix for a sample **Move In/Move Out Inspection** form.

A schedule of the fees charged for various cleaning and replacement services can be prepared in advance. This fee schedule for move out costs can be made part of the lease agreement. Your fees should be based on actual costs, not some arbitrary amount. Here are some examples:

Cleaning Fees		**Replacement Fees**	
Refrigerator	$30.00	Light Bulbs	$ 1.00
Oven, Stove & Hood	$40.00	Door & Mailbox Keys	$ 35.00
Tub/Shower	$25.00	Doors (Wooden)	$100.00
Carpet Cleaning	$80.00	Carpet Repair	$100.00
Trash removal	$40.00	Doors (Glass)	$165.00
Sinks, Cabinets	$25.00	Window Screens	$ 40.00

This is a small, sample list. Each landlord must evaluate his/her property and make a fee list that fits his/her needs. Including a list of fees charged in the lease agreement may limit disputes over security deposit fees. It will take some work to make sure the fees are adequate and fair, but headaches and haggling may be eliminated by this effort.

How to determine security deposit amount

In a perfect world you could collect first month's rent, last month's rent and a security deposit in advance. If you can do this by all means do. It is most often the custom to charge one month's rent as a security deposit but I strongly recommend charging more. Frequently, the tenant will leave without paying the last month's rent. If you require only one month's rent as a deposit, you will have no money to pay for any repairs needed, unless the tenant pays voluntarily. Requiring between one and two months' rent as a deposit leaves you covered. If the monthly rent is $750.00 you would want a security deposit of, at the very least, $750.00. If your tenant has the funds available, $1325.00 to $1500.00 is reasonable.

If the lease is month-to-month your security deposit should be one month's rent plus $75.00. You also should collect the usual non-refundable rental application fee, pet deposit and cleaning fee. Charge a key deposit of $2.00 to $10.00 per key (refundable only if all keys are returned to you).

Do not rent to someone who cannot pay at least one month's rent as a security deposit; they will surely not have reserve funds to pay any damage fees.

Make sure the security deposit monies are in a special security deposit account and not in the account where you deposit your rent monies. You do not pay taxes on fees earmarked for security deposits and you most likely do not want to give a tenant your business checking account number.

Non-refundable administrative and cleaning fees

- Include a clean up, painting and administrative fee of $40.00 to $100.00 in the move-in fee. Each time you rent the unit add this fee, which is not included in the security deposit, up front.
- Require a non-refundable application fee of $30.00 to $75.00 to cover your costs of checking credit, employment and rental history and any administrative procedures.
- Set a key deposit of $2.00 to $10.00 with the key provided by you. If all keys are returned you will refund this deposit. If locks have been changed you will not refund the key deposit as you will have keys that don't work.

For this example I have chosen to charge $750.00/month for rent, 1½ rents for the security deposit, $50.00 for the rental application fees, $40.00 for the cleaning fee and $5.00 for each key. Your renter will need to pay you the following, in cash, cashier's check or money order, as move in fees:

Rental Application fee	$ 50.00
Cleaning fee	40.00
Security Deposit	1325.00
Rent, first month's	750.00
Key Deposit (2@ $5.00)	10.00
	$2175.00

The rental application fee is collected when the rental application is presented to you for verification. Cleaning fees, the security deposit, first month's rent and key deposit must be paid to you in cash, money order or cashier's check *before* you give the tenant access to the unit.

Do not give any keys to the tenant or allow any items into your rental property until everything is complete and you have all of your fees in hand. If you need motivation go rent the movie *Pacific Heights.* You'll understand.

Do not accept a personal check for the initial move in fees; once the tenant is in possession of the unit you will have to institute a dispossessory proceeding to remove him/her if s/he will not voluntarily leave. Also make sure that the lease and move-in inspection report are signed before allowing the tenant to move in.

CHAPTER FOUR

The Move Out

Notification of move out

As the end of the lease agreement draws near, your tenant should notify you of his/her intent to vacate. Prior to the notice date, the landlord can provide a simple form letter for the tenant to use. For example, if the tenant is required to give you thirty days notice supply the **Notice of Intention to Vacate** 45 to sixty days before the expiration date of the lease.

Advise the departing tenant what s/he can do to ensure that all deposit money is refunded. Many problems arise because the landlord has not communicated his/her expectations to the tenant. It will be helpful to you and the tenant if you take the time to explain your move out procedure. Send the tenant a letter along the lines of the following to make your expectations clear.

Acme Apartment
1000 Any Street, Goodtown, USA
June 1, 1993

Dear Departing Tenant:

We have received notice and understand that you are moving. We hate to lose you.

It should comfort you to know that Georgia law requires landlords to inspect vacated property within three days and to refund all security deposits due within thirty days. It has long been my policy to comply with the law.

I wish to point out that security deposit funds will be held to pay for the following defects, if any: damages caused by tenant, tenant's relatives or guests, pet damage, unpaid rents or late fees, utilities and unusual cleaning fees.

If you leave your unit reasonably clean and undamaged, your deposit will be refunded in full. In addition, I have elected to give you the interest earned on your security deposit as my thanks for your consideration of my property.

"Reasonably clean" means to leave the unit as clean as you would if you knew your best friend or favorite relative were going to move in after you. I expect you to clean the appliances, stove hood, and cabinets inside and out. Clean showers, tubs, toilets, sinks, mirrors and medicine cabinets with a non-abrasive disinfectant. Dust the ceilings, baseboards, window sills, mini-blinds and closet shelving. Wash the kitchen and bathroom walls and spot clean the walls in the other rooms. Wash the light fixtures and windows inside and out.

Vacuum the floors. Scrub all tile floors. Sweep the entry, patio, deck, storage area, and driveway (garage). Remove all personal belongings and dispose of all trash.

DO NOT clean the draperies, shampoo carpets or wax the floors. I prefer to do those cleaning chores myself and I will not deduct anything from your deposit for them.

"Reasonably undamaged" means that items which I have supplied should not be missing or broken. This includes light bulbs. There should be no new burns, cracks, chips or holes in the dwelling or its furnishings and the paint on the walls should show only normal wear and tear. Please do not remove anything you have attached to the walls or ceilings without first talking to me. Please try to avoid nicking the paint on the banisters, halls and doorways as you move things out.

After you have returned the keys, I will inspect the unit for cleanliness and damage. If no defects exists, I will refund all deposits owed to you, plus interest, via U.S. mail. Make sure you have provided your forwarding address.

I expect you to be moved out completely by _____ 19___.
I would appreciate hearing from you if your moving plans change.
Good luck in your new home.
Sincerely,

Margaret Manager

The move out inspection

Once the tenant is out, you must make a move-out inspection. Inspect the dwelling and document all deficiencies on the Move-In/Move Out Inspection form. Below is the required procedure according to Georgia law:

1. Upon termination of the lease or surrender and acceptance, whichever occurs later, the landlord must conduct an inspection within three working days. A comprehensive list of all damages noted must be written and signed by the landlord. The charges made against the security deposit must be noted and documented as well. The list of damages and charges signed by the landlord must be presented to the tenant. Tenant is then entitled to inspect the property within five days after s/he has moved out.

2. Tenant must sign the move out inspection accepting the landlord's inspection report and acknowledging the amount landlord withheld from the security deposit. If the tenant dissents s/he must do so in writing. Tenant must then sue landlord to recover any portion of the security deposit that the tenant believes was improperly withheld.

Have the inspection form ready for the tenant on the third day after the unit is vacated, as provided by Georgia law. Calculate charges and repair costs fairly.

Dated before and after photos will help substantiate your claim for repair fees. Make sure all invoices for work done are dated and signed by the contractor who did the work. If you anticipate a fight with the tenant document everything you can. Have your contractors write a description of the damages before they begin fixing them.

If the tenant vacates without notice, the landlord must make his/her final inspection within reasonable time after discovering the dwelling vacant. "Reasonable time" is an arbitrary term and can be applied as the judge or jury sees fit. As soon as you discover that your property has been abandoned, inspect it. Be sure that you document the date you found your property empty and the date you conducted your inspection. After this inspection the usual rules, as outlined in this chapter, apply.

Returning the security deposit

Should the tenant give proper notice and vacate the property without owing any rent or fees for damage the landlord must return the security deposit, in full, within thirty days of the lease termination or surrender and acceptance of the premises, whichever occurs later. If the landlord fails to provide written statements concerning the reasons for not fully refunding deposits within the time periods specified s/he forfeits all right to withhold any portion of the security deposit or to bring an action against the tenant for damages to the premises.

Many tenants do not understand the strict law governing how their landlord must handle the security deposit. If the landlord does not properly refund the security deposit s/he may be penalized and will be fined. The penalty is specified by Georgia law as three times the security deposit plus legal fees incurred by the tenant. It may be beneficial for you to explain this to the tenant. When s/he understands that you are bound by law to return the security deposit, this knowledge may help to limit their temptation to ignore the last month's rent. The departing tenant may even clean the place if s/he knows the deposit money will be refunded. As incentive you may remind your tenant that you intend to pay him/her any interest that has accrued on the security deposit if the unit is left clean and undamaged.

Please note that pet deposits and advance rent (first and last month's rent) are considered under the Security Deposit Act; they are refundable fees. Application fees and move in cleaning fees are not considered under the Security Deposit Act; they are non-refundable fees. Of course any repairs, late fees, pet fees, and unpaid rent may be deducted from the deposit. Please remember that last month's rent is last month's rent. It cannot be used for anything else.

Make sure you can justify all monies that you withhold for repair of damages. Receipts for work done or purchased items are the best proof that you withheld the correct amount from the security deposit. The court will not accept projected or arbitrary amounts. If landlord can prove an honest mistake or bona fide error s/he is then only liable for the actual deposit.

The landlord is required to mail the security deposit funds to the last known address or new address provided by the tenant via first class mail. If returned undeliverable and the landlord is unable to locate the tenant by "reasonable effort" within ninety days, the security deposit then belongs to the landlord. Reasonable effort will include calling the tenant's place of employment, contacting the references given on the rental application, contacting any relatives you know of and asking the post office to provide you the tenant's forwarding address. Don't make careless errors or fail to exercise reasonable care in locating the tenant. It could cost you a lot of money and time.

CHAPTER FIVE

How To Legally Evict Your Tenant

Georgia law and the steps to legal eviction

The only legal means by which a landlord can evict a tenant and his/her personal property from rented premises is called a dispossession. A dispossessory proceeding is the legal process initiated by a landlord to reclaim his/her rental property and cancel the lease agreement. In other words, it is the legal term for eviction.

Please note that this book is written for *residential* property only. When trying to evict a commercial tenant there are other rules and regulations that apply. They are not covered in this text.

Section Eight or any other subsidized housing is governed by federal and HUD guidelines and *is not* covered in this text. Do not use this text as a panacea for *all* landlord solutions.

The proper reasons for eviction in Georgia:

- Non-payment of rent
- Breach of the lease
- Failure to surrender the premises at the end of the lease term (tenant holding over)
- Tenancy at will
- Tenancy at sufferance

If you are squeamish about courts, fear not. This chapter will give you the low down on the proceedings and walk you through step by step.

Title 44, chapter seven of the Code of Georgia provides the basis for most of this chapter. If you have any questions regarding the law consult a lawyer or the code for more information. Make sure the lawyer whose services you seek is skilled in handling tenant/landlord cases. (See page 61 for information on choosing a lawyer.)

Before beginning your first legal proceeding you may want to try one of these kinder, gentler eviction methods:

1. Ask your tenant to leave. Offer to terminate the lease. S/he may have wanted to move, but perhaps feared retaliation on your part. In some cases it is much less expensive to have your tenant move out, thereby avoiding dispossessory fees and time spent in court.

2. Offer the tenant an incentive to move such as paying for the moving truck and crew yourself. It may be lack of funds that keeps him/her in your rental unit. The moving expense may actually be less than lost rent and court fees. It's worth $100.00 to get some folks out.

3. Openly photograph any obvious violation of the rental agreement such as unruly guests, trash on the lawn, etc. Make sure the tenant sees you taking pictures. When the tenant asks, "What the hell are you doing?" you can sweetly say "Gathering evidence for my dispossessory case against you." It just might be the motivation s/he needs to move out. You can save the photos for evidence if you need them later on.

4. It may be helpful to notify the co-signer that his/her co-signee is behind in the rent or has caused damage to your property. The co-signer may have influence where you do not and may be able to convince the tenant to pay up or move out. You can ask the co-signer to pay the past due rent.

If any of these methods work you will want to have the tenant sign a letter agreeing to terminate his/her lease effective immediately. Have the tenant sign it on the spot. Both parties (the landlord and the tenant) must agree to cancel the lease.

This may be done at any time during the term of the lease if both parties agree. Be willing to terminate the lease only if you can get those tenants out of your property before rent is due again. Otherwise it defeats the purpose of saving you money because you don't want to be out more than one month's rent.

If the tenant will not agree to quickly vacate your property, you'll be better off with a judgment from the court for unpaid rent, late fees and filing fees. However, if the tenant is judgment proof (does not have enough assets to cover the cost of your repairs or unpaid rent) you simply want them out of your property as soon as humanly possible. Canceling the lease and getting them out of the property before the rent is due again may be the best way to limit your losses.

If this approach fails, you must initiate a dispossessory proceeding against your tenant.

In order to legally evict your tenant you must perform each of the tasks detailed below. If you fail to perform any step you may invalidate your proceeding and have your case thrown out of court. Do not make the mistake of thinking that you are special and deserving of short cuts. You are not. Any false claims or errors may result in your being charged with a misdemeanor. Make sure you faithfully execute each step.

Course of events when entering into dispossessory proceedings

This is a general description of the steps you will need to take for each kind of eviction. A thorough explanation of each step follows this general outline.

For non-payment of rent:
- Send a strict compliance notice.
- Demand possession the day rent is late.
- File a dispossessory affidavit.

For breach or violation of rental agreement:
- As soon as breach or violation occurs, write a letter demanding a cure of the breach within ten days.
- If the tenant fails to cure the breach, on the eleventh day write a letter that states "Your lease is terminated because..." and demand immediate possession of the property.
- If the dwelling is not vacated within 24 hours, file a dispossessory affidavit.

For tenant at will who is holding over:
- Write a letter giving the tenant sixty days notice that you are terminating the tenancy.
- When the sixty days have passed and the tenant has not vacated, the landlord must demand immediate possession and wait 24 hours.
- File a dispossessory affidavit.

For tenant at sufferance who is holding over:
- Upon or after expiration of the lease agreement send a letter demanding immediate possession. Wait 24 hours.
- If your demand is refused, file a dispossessory affidavit.

Step one: strict compliance or cure of breach notice

The strict compliance notice is a letter from you, the landlord, to the tenant stating when rent is due, how much is due and that late payments will not be accepted.

If you have accepted late payments in the past you have given up your right to demand strict compliance to the lease provision requiring timely payment. Regardless of what may be stated in your lease, any time you accept rent money from the tenant after the due date you waive your right to demand strict compliance!

You may reinstate your right to insist upon prompt payment of future rental installments by notifying the tenant, in writing, that strict compliance to the term of the lease will be insisted upon in the future.

This letter must be delivered to the tenant as described in the notice section of the lease agreement. In fact, all notices described in this section must be delivered as you indicated in the lease agreement. You may supplement the method of delivery with other verifiable means such as registered or certified mail, certification of mailing, etc.

After this notice is given you must insist on timely payment before you have grounds to evict for non-payment of the rent.

If you accept any portion of the rent beyond the due date after sending this notice, you must once again re-establish your right to demand timely payment. Make no exceptions. Accept the rent when due and not later. Otherwise you will be constantly writing and sending letters demanding strict compliance.

Sample strict compliance notice:

Acme Apartments
1000 Any Street, Goodtown, USA
June 1, 1993

Ms. Tammy Tenant   **Via Certified Mail**
9999 Happy Street   *(use method described in your lease)*
Goodtown, USA

Re: Lease of 9999 Happy Street, Goodtown, USA

Dear Ms. Tenant:

According to the written lease between yourself and Acme Apartments, rent is due in the amount of $750.00 per month on the first day of each month. Please be advised that although rent may have been accepted after the date due in the past, beginning June 1, 1993 the terms of the lease will be strictly enforced and rent is expected to be paid on or before the first day of each month.

Your cooperation is appreciated.

Sincerely,

Margaret Manager
Landlord

When you discover a breach of any lease provision you must notify the tenant of the breach, demand a cure and provide time for the cure to be made.

Sample letter demanding cure for breach of lease:

Acme Apartments
1000 Any Street, Goodtown, USA
June 1, 1993

Ms. Tammy Tenant   **Via Certified Mail**
9999 Happy Street   *(use method described in your lease)*
Goodtown, USA

Re: Lease of 9999 Happy Street, Anytown, USA

Dear Ms. Tenant:

You are in violation of the following provisions of your lease agreement:

list any breach here.

You are hereby notified that the above breach(es) must be corrected within ten days of receipt of this letter.

Failure to act on your part will result in termination of your lease. Your cooperation is appreciated.

Sincerely,

Margaret Manager
Landlord

This completes the first step. Now you must wait for your renter to be late with the rent payment or fail to cure the breach. When s/he fails to pay rent when due or fails to cure the breach proceed with your demand for possession.

Step two: demand for possession

Demand for possession of the property must be made before you file dispossessory papers with the court regardless of the reason you seek to dispossess the tenant.

Let's say it is 5:00 pm on the second day of the month (or whatever day of that month you deem rent to be late), and you have not received your rental payment. It is time to demand possession in writing.

If you have not waived your right to insist upon strict compliance by accepting rental payments past the date they were due, you do not have to demand rent; you only need to demand possession. The *demand for possession* is a legal formality which gives the tenant the opportunity to voluntarily move out of your unit.

Remember, if you were nice and accepted rent after the due date, even once, you must demand payment of rent along with your demand for possession. You must also give the tenant time (I suggest one to five days) to pay the rent. If s/he pays the rent, it's over until the next monthly payment is late. The last paragraph in the sample demand letter for non-payment of rent, "Demand is further made for payment of the rental installment..." will avoid any question of there being strict compliance notice and re-establishes your right to demand such in the future.

Demand for possession for non-payment of rent:

Acme Apartments
1000 Any Street, Goodtown, USA
June 1, 1993

Ms. Tammy Tenant						**Via certified mail**
9999 Happy Street					*(Use method described in your lease.)*
Goodtown, USA

Re: Lease of 9999 Happy Street, Goodtown, USA

Dear Ms. Tenant:
You have failed to pay your rent when due. Unless you remit in cash or certified funds the amount of $_____, by June 6, 1993, (five days from date of letter) I shall take the appropriate legal action.

If you fail to make the above described payment you must remove all of your personal property, return all keys and surrender said premises to: _____*owner, landlord, etc.*_____ by June 6, 1993. Demand for possession of 9999 Happy Street is hereby made.

Demand is further made for payment of the rental installment on or before the first of each month, in advance, commencing July 1, 1993.

This matter requires your immediate attention.

Sincerely,

Margaret Manager
Owner

Demand for possession to a tenant holding over:
It is important that you understand the difference between tenancy at will and tenancy at sufferance when you are trying to dispossess someone who is holding over, in other words, remaining in possesion of the property beyond the term of the lease.

If your tenant does not give proper notice to exercise his/her option to renew the lease agreement, the day after the lease expires s/he becomes a tenant at sufferance, which means s/he is occupying your property *without* your permission.

If you accept any rent payment or infer that it is all right for him/her to remain in your dwelling, s/he becomes a tenant at will. This means s/he is residing in your dwelling *with* your permission but does not have a specified term for this tenancy.

If you can prove a tenancy at sufferance, no notice other than the demand for possession is required. On the other hand, if you have allowed this to turn into a tenancy at will you must give the tenant sixty days notice that the lease is terminated and then you must wait those sixty days before you can demand possession. However, if the tenant at will is behind in the rent payment, you may file a dispossessory for non-payment of rent and aviod the sixty day notice altogether.

Acme Apartments
1000 Any Street, Goodtown, USA
June 1, 1993

Ms. Tammy Tenant**Via certified mail**
9999 Happy Street*(Use method described in your lease.)*
Goodtown, USA

Re: Lease of 9999 Happy Street, Goodtown, USA

Dear Ms. Tenant:

You are in possession of the above referenced premises beyond the term of your lease. Demand for immediate possession is hereby made.

Sincerely,

Margaret Manager
Owner

THE LANDLORD'S PRIMER

Demand for possession for failure to cure breach of the lease:

You have notified the tenant that a breach exists, have given her/him time to cure said breach and the tenant has failed to respond. You now demand possession of the property.

Acme Apartments
1000 Any Street, Goodtown, USA
June 1, 1993

Ms. Tammy Tenant   **Via certified mail**
9999 Happy Street   *(Use method described in your lease.)*
Goodtown, USA

Re: Lease of 9999 Happy Street, Goodtown, USA

Dear Ms. Tenant:
Your lease agreement is hereby terminated. You have failed to correct the lease violations cited in my letter of _____, 19___.
You must vacate the unit and return the keys on or before_____, 19___. If you fail to vacate the apartment by the above date, I will begin eviction proceedings to obtain legal possession of your unit.
 Demand for immediate possession is hereby made.

Sincerely,

Margaret Manager
Owner

 In all cases, demand for possession must be made by the owner, the owner's agent or manager, attorney at law or attorney in fact.

 Demand for possession must be made by the landlord and refused by the tenant before the landlord can file the affidavit that starts the eviction process. You must use the delivery method outlined in your lease agreement.

 If you want delivery of the notice verified, it is best to send it registered or certified mail and request a signed receipt. When using first class mail take the envelope to the post office and request a certificate of mailing from the postal worker. Fill it out and the postal employee will affix proper validation. There is a small charge for this certificate. It does not provide a return receipt or notice of delivery.

 The tenant is legally entitled to respond to the demand for possesion. Wait the number of days specified in your letter, usually one to ten. If the tenant has not vacated your property and/or the rent has not been paid you can begin dispossessory proceedings when the time limit has expired. However, if you are demanding possession from a tenant holding over, you only need to wait 24 hours after delivery of demand for possession and then file the dispossessory affidavit.

 If you have not waived your right to insist on prompt rental payment you are entitled to refuse payments which are presented late and you may proceed to evict the tenant on the grounds of failure to pay rent when due. Most courts in Georgia will not allow you to continue with the eviction if you accept rent after filing the dispossessory affidavit.

Refuse late payment or any offer of money. Holding or depositing the rental funds may signify acceptance and you will no longer be able to dispossess the tenant for non-payment of rent. Do not hold the tenant's payment or present it to your bank. Return the payment immediately with a letter that states the following:

Sample refusal of payment:

Acme Apartments
1000 Any Street, Goodtown, USA
June 1, 1993

Ms. Tammy Tenant **Via certified mail**
9999 Happy Street *(Use method described in your lease.)*
Goodtown, USA

Re: Lease of 9999 Happy Street, Goodtown, USA

Dear Ms. Tenant:

Enclosed is your check # _____ for $_____. The offer to pay rent is late and is refused.

Demand for possession of the premises is hereby made.

Your cooperation is appreciated.

Sincerely,

Margaret Manager
Landlord

Keep a copy of the check and this letter in your file. Making a partial payment is a common trick that tenants use to stop the dispossessory and buy more time. Don't fall for it. If you accept any payment, full or partial, you cannot proceed again until the next rental payment is past due.

NOTE: If you are filing the dispossessory for a tenant holding over you may accept rental payments after you have brought dispossessory proceedings. The landlord is entitled to rental payments until possession is delivered in cases involving tenants holding over. Do not confuse this. You may accept payment of rent after the dispossessory warrant has been filed only if your tenant is holding over. **Do not accept payment if you are seeking to evict your tenant for non-payment of rent.**

Dispossessory proceedings

If the tenant moves out after receiving your demand for possession you need go no further with the dispossessory proceeding. However, if the tenant left owing you money, you will have to file a lawsuit to collect. See chapter seven.

Dispossessory proceedings cannot be instituted until you have sent a demand for possession and that demand has been refused. Do not file the dispossessory before you demand possession. This is a procedural error and if it is brought to the judge's attention the case will be dismissed.

If you have demanded possession and that demand has been refused your next step is to file an affidavit in the county where the property is located. Because of the high volume of dispossessory proceedings most courts have pre-printed affidavit forms for you to fill out.

Dispossessory actions can be filed in State or Magistrate Court. Ask for the dispossessory clerk in your county and you will be automatically be directed to one or the other. However, if your claim is greater than $5,000.00 you cannot file in Magistrate Court.

Magistrate Court is a bit less formal and is designed to assist *pro se* litigants (those who do not have a lawyer and choose to represent themselves). It is the "People's Court" of Georgia.

Make a practice run to the courthouse and familiarize yourself with the physical set up, and the filing procedures. Make friends with everyone who works there. Don't appear hostile or rude; it's not the clerks' fault that you rented to a non-paying tenant and they can provide answers to your questions. I have found the clerks to be very knowledgeable and quite helpful.

Sitting through one or two sessions of dispossessory court is eye opening. It will give you a great deal of confidence when you see how things go. If your reasons for seeking dispossession are legitimate and you have followed the guidelines for seeking this remedy you will most likely win your case, since the judge simply rules on the evidence presented.

Here are the questions that you will have to answer on the dispossessory affidavit form:

PLAINTIFF'S NAME AND ADDRESS: you, the landlord.

DEFENDANT'S NAME AND ADDRESS: your tenant. The person(s) whose name(s) and signature(s) appears on the lease agreement must be named in this section. Make sure you spell their names correctly. If you list someone whose name is not on the lease, the court may throw out your case or complicate matters by adding more defendants to it.

REASON FOR FILING:
1) Tenant has failed to pay rent;
2) Tenant is holding the premises over and beyond the term of the lease;
3) Said tenant is a tenant at sufferance; or
4) "Other grounds" as may be considered a breach or violation of the lease agreement. (Make sure you can prove your allegations. If you lose your case the tenant may stay in your dwelling and can sue you for all foreseeable damages caused by wrongful misconduct of the landlord.)

PLAINTIFF PRAYS OR DEMANDS:
1) Possession of the premises;
2) The rents past due, calculated daily based on a thirty day month; and
3) Any late or other fees. Make sure you have figured these amounts honestly and correctly. If you underestimate them you will have limited the amount

the court can award to you. If you overestimate them you are making fraudulent claims and could end up on the wrong end of this action. Be careful.

Sign and date the affidavit and hand it back to the clerk. The clerk will check the document, ask you questions, ask you to swear to the document and collect a filing fee. This will cost $45.00 in Fulton County for one defendant and $8.00 for an additional defendant. In DeKalb County, the fee is $36.00 and in Cobb County, $50.00 for one defendant and $70.00 for two. These fees were in force as of February 1993; fee increases will most certainly occur.

The affidavit must be sworn to before a judge, clerk, deputy or magistrate of the court. If your document is not properly sworn to it is not valid. You will have wasted precious time if the tenant brings this to the attention of the court. While you scratch your head and restart the dispossessory proceedings your tenant is still living rent free in your dwelling.

You must follow these steps correctly. Mistakes can cause your case to be filed incorrectly or thrown out of court. If you knowingly make false claims you could be charged with a misdemeanor. Read and reread this section until you understand it. Go to the courthouse in the county where your property is located and ask the clerk to walk you through the process. Be mindful that s/he may be busy. If so, ask when a good time would be for you to come back. You'll only have to do this once or twice and then you will know what procedure you must follow.

Service of the summons

Serving the papers, or *service of process* is how the defendant (tenant) is notified that a lawsuit has been filed against him/her. A defendant must be notified by summons and given time to answer the summons.

After you have filed your affidavit, a dispossessory warrant is sent to the marshal, constable or sheriff to serve. You may go to their office and find out how many days it will be before they can serve your summons. It is generally three to five days from the date you filed. Be nice to these people, as they are the ones who will execute the writ of possession you so dearly want that grants you legal possession of your property.

Make sure it is clear on your affidavit where the property is located. If the street address is not adequate, give more detailed information so the sheriff can find the place and properly serve the papers to the tenant.

After the summons has been served the marshal, sheriff or constable will mail a copy to you. This will give the date of service to the tenant and the last date the tenant may appear to answer the summons. This date is important since it's when you can find out whether or not the tenant answered.

This is the approximate time frame: If a marshal serves the summons to the tenant on the third of the month, the tenant is instructed to answer (appear in the Clerk's Office) on or before the tenth. You may get a copy or verbal report of the tenant's answer from the clerk on the eleventh day of the month, and not before.

Defendant's answer

An *answer* is the tenant's response to the allegations you have made in your affidavit.

Your tenant is required to answer the summons, in person, within seven days of the date of service. If the seventh day is a Saturday, Sunday or legal holiday, s/he may answer the next business day. Your copy of the served summons will indicate the last day the tenant can answer. Call the morning after that last date or wait for your copy to arrive in the mail.

If the tenant does not answer

If your tenant fails to answer the summons s/he is in default. Default is an automatic win for you because the defendant failed to answer your summons.

You may get a writ of possession from the clerk of the court, take it immediately to the Marshal's Office and arrange for them to supervise the eviction of your tenant. The marshal only supervises the eviction. You must provide the labor for the physical removal of the tenant and his/her belongings. You will be able to regain possession of your property in a week or so.

If the tenant does not answer and the marshal has served the papers by posting (nail and mail), not in person, you cannot collect any money judgment from the dispossessory proceeding. You must file a separate small claims or collection law suit. The procedure for this is explained in chapter seven.

If you suspect that the tenant will not answer and you want to be awarded unpaid rent and fees, ask the marshal, constable, or sheriff to deliver the summons in person. You can indicate "personal service" in large handwritten letters on the request for service. Ask the clerk where to write this request on the form.

If the tenant answers

The tenant must appear in person to respond to the dispossessory summons. Regardless of what the tenant's reply is, a court date is set within seven to 14 days. You will receive a copy of the tenant's answer in the mail. If you can't wait you may pick it up from the clerk.

Georgia law gives the tenant free reign in the answer department. The tenant can say anything s/he wants to say. In fact, DeKalb and Cobb Countys' answer forms consist of blank lines.

If the summons is in some way defective the tenant must say so in her/his answer or must file a motion with the court. Failure to point out the defect amounts to giving up the right to argue about or question it. In theory then, you might slide by if you goof but if your tenant is determined to oppose you, s/he will notice a problem with the summons. For your own protection make sure you have completed the affidavit honestly and accurately.

If the tenant denies any of the allegations, those issues are heard and ruled upon by the court. Allegations which are not denied are presumed to be admitted.

Since Georgia gives the tenant such leeway in answering your summons, I cannot predict all possible answers. The following are some of the most common:

a. *I am unable to pay the rent.* The tenant answers that s/he cannot pay rent because s/he is out of a job, has unexpected financial burdens, became ill and could not work, etc. This is not an adequate legal defense. The court will have great empathy but will generally rule in your favor. The judge will order the tenant to pay back rent, late fees and daily rent accruing up to the date on which they actually move out and order the tenant to vacate the property within ten days. This is called a "Motion for Judgment on the Pleadings".

The landlord cannot take *any* action, threaten or harass the tenant within these ten days. Any threat or harassment is illegal. Under Georgia law a judgment cannot be enforced for ten days, which is why the judge gives the tenant this time to move out.

If you feel that your property will be further damaged say so to the judge while you are in court. The judge will remind the tenant that s/he can go to jail for willfully damaging your property. It's pretty effective.

Using our hypothetical case, ten days worth of rent would be $750.00 (the monthy rent) divided by thirty or $25.00 per day. Make sure you indicate the daily rent correctly on your original summons, as this is the figure the court will use to determine your award. If the summons contains mistakes you may be required to refile. Guess where your tenant is for the duration? That's right, in your property and not paying the rent.

When ten days have passed a writ of possession is issued which transfers possession back to you, the landlord, and cancels the lease. This writ instructs the marshal, constable or sheriff to allow removal of the tenant and any personal property from your dwelling. The tenant is under no further obligation to make the rental payments, and must be out by midnight on the tenth day. Otherwise, the marshal will approve the eviction.

b. *My landlord has failed to repair the property. This failure has lowered its value or resulted in other damages more than the rent claimed.*

The tenant must have complained and notified the landlord before the dispossessory warrant was served and the tenant must be able to prove that failure to make repairs has devalued the rental amount to the point that his/her damages equal or exceed the delinquent rental payment.

If the tenant proves his/her claim you will have to accept the devalued amount, as determined by the judge, as rental payment.

If the dispossessory action is based on the tenant holding over, repairs do not enter into the issue and will not be considered as a defense for holding over.

You cannot avoid your responsibility to make repairs. If your tenant makes a request for legitimate repairs, honor it.

c. *I deny the claim and I do not owe any rent.* The landlord must prove that the rent payment has not been received. Make sure you document payments carefully with written receipts and copies of payment instruments. If you have accepted even $1.00 toward the payment of the past due rent you could lose your case.

d. *I have not received prior notice.* Keep copies of all correspondence. All documents' receipt can be confirmed by certificate of mailing, return receipt mail or the personal signature of the person accepting the notice. I have seen cases thrown out because the marshal did not mail the tenant's copy of the summons the same day one was posted to the tenant's door.

e. *My landlord would not accept my rent and the cost of this warrant.* If your tenant pays the rent and the cost of the dispossessory warrant within seven days of receiving the summons the landlord is required to accept this late payment only *one* time in any twelve month period.

If you have already done this once in a twelve month period, you don't have to do it again. Refuse the rent payment and bring to court documentation (your copy of the first summons and the tenant's answer, the check and the date paid) that you have already accepted late payment once in a twelve month period.

f. *My landlord failed to make requested repairs, and I made these repairs that cost $_____.* The tenant will have to document that s/he gave you proper written notice and the cost of the repair work to be done. If you have failed to make necessary repairs the tenant will be allowed to "repair and deduct". You can question any extravagant cost and refute it with estimates of your own, but you will have to accept paid receipts in lieu of rent in this case.

The tenant may not use this as a defense after you have instituted dispossessory proceedings. If you have not been previously notified that a repair was required and the tenant brings this up *after* being served a dispossessory summons, the tenant has no case and repair receipts will not be allowed as substitution for rent.

If you are not certain how to proceed when you receive the tenant's answer, consult a lawyer or your apartment owner's association.

Warning

Do not sit around complacently while you are waiting for the case to go to court. You need to use this time to gather, organize and prepare a data file containing *all* information pertinent to this case. Include any complaints from other tenants, documented infraction of rules, payment record, a copy of the lease agreement, etc. This will be your basis for bringing and proving your suit.

Make sure all information is accurate and can be verified. Do not attempt any slippery tactics. It makes you look bad and the judge is clever enough to spot a con when s/he sees one. Don't forget that s/he sits up there every day and listens to contrived stories.

Most of the time the tenant will not bring anything to the court room — neither a receipt for payment of the rent, nor a copy of the lease. Thorough preparation is your key to quick relief.

If you are proceeding for non-payment of rent make sure you can document that the tenant has not paid. The burden of proof rests with the plaintiff. The court will not tolerate anything but hard evidence. Bring your receipt book (make sure each receipt clearly indicates which month the payment covers), ledger cards and copies of checks, money orders, or other payment instruments that the tenant has previously presented for payment.

In an action for nonpayment of the rent, the tenant is allowed to pay to the landlord, within seven days of the date the tenant was served the summons, all rents allegedly owed plus the cost of the dispossessory warrant one time in any twelve month period. This payment is a complete defense of the action. Georgia landlords are required to accept this payment from a tenant after a dispossessory summons has been issued *only* once in any twelve month period. Do not accept any payment until the tenant has been served the dispossessory warrant. This provision must have been met before you can successfully dispossess the tenant. Keep in mind you are only required to do this once in any twelve month period.

Tenant tricks to watch out for:

- *Money order receipts:* Make sure the money order was payable to the landlord. Tenants will produce these receipts and a trace will show that the money order was made out to the tenant or someone other than the landlord.
- *False medical excuses.* Call the hospital or doctor. Check the excuse carefully; you may notice altered dates or reasons. This is a classic way to obtain sympathy from the judge.
- *Constructive eviction—i.e. your tenant claims that s/he has moved out because the unit is unfit to live in.* The unit must really be uninhabitable, not merely uncomfortable, for a tenant to legally perform a constructive eviction. Have photos and documentation available to disprove the tenant's claim that the dwelling is uninhabitable.
- *Bankruptcy.* A bankruptcy petition automatically stops your action to dispossess or collect rent arrearage. Do your best to regain possession of your property before the tenant files bankruptcy.
- *Mixed up months.* It is imperative that you keep clear, concise records to indicate when and for what month rent was paid. If the tenant does not pay in April, pays in May and June, the receipt must indicate that the May payment was applied to April's rent and June payment was applied to May's rent —leaving June unpaid. You cannot evict for non-payment of rent unless the tenant has not paid in the month in which you file a dispossessory.

In this case, the tenant will show the judge checks dated May 1 and June 1. You will have to present evidence to explain what happened. Do not let your tenant get behind in rent payments.

If the court is unable to set a hearing date or rule in a dispossessory case within two weeks from the date the tenant was served the summons, ask the court to order the tenant to pay any rent due into the *registry of the court,* which is an escrow account controlled by the court.

Your day in court

PREPARE! PREPARE! PREPARE! PREPARE! PREPARE! PREPARE! The only way to present an accurate picture of your claim(s) is to have documents supporting your position. Prepare your case *fully* in advance to increase your chances of winning. It is best to be over prepared. There is no need to add to any anxieties you may be feeling about the legal process by looking foolish and disorganized.

If you cannot *prove* your claims do not file a lawsuit. Hard evidence is what wins cases, not unsubstantiated claims.

The Magistrate Court is designed to handle cases by legal amateurs or *pro se*. *Pro se* means you are representing yourself and no lawyer is involved. This court is very tolerant of litigants (people involved in a lawsuit) who are not familiar with courtroom procedure. I have seen the judge patiently explain the process to all parties in a law suit.

It may give you peace of mind to consult an attorney before you proceed on your own. There are many dedicated lawyers willing to give simple advice regarding your case and the advisability of proceeding on your own.

Make sure you bring the following items to court with you on the day your case will be heard:

- The lease
- Payment records
- Any correspondence, notices or complaints between tenant and landlord.
- Physical evidence such as a piece of damaged carpet, etc.
- Any document in which the tenant admits fault
- Estimates for repair costs, cleaning receipts, etc.
- Voluntary witnesses.

Organize your evidence logically and chronologically. Practice your presentation. Make it complete but brief. Good pre-trial preparation is most important. It may be helpful to write an outline to follow when presenting your case:

- Your honor, my name is Margaret Manager and I own the property located at 9999 Happy Street that is currently leased by Ms. Tammy Tenant.
- On July 7, I discovered damage to my property. I photographed the damage and sent a letter to Ms. Tenant citing the damage and demanding repair within ten days.

- On July 20, I posted a **Notice of Intention to Enter** for the purpose of inspecting demanded repairs.
- On July 21, I inspected the property and took photos of the unrepaired damage. Ms. Tenant did not repair the property as requested. I terminated her lease and demanded immediate possession of the property.
- Demand for possession was disregarded and on July 26, I filed the dispossessory affidavit.

The judge may stop you to ask questions or ask for a piece of evidence. S/he will look at the lease, look over your other evidence and then hear the other side.

You will have the opportunity to respond to the claims made by the defendant. Wait until the judge asks for your comments.

When you appear in court please be aware of courtroom etiquette and procedure. It is very important to arrive on time. The judge calls the roll. If you are not present when your name is called, you have defaulted and your case will be dismissed because you were absent.

An observation day will give you the most insight on how things are handled in the court where you have filed your case. Make it a point to go and observe dispossessory court proceedings before you undertake any legal action. You can see courtroom dynamics, other litigants and the judge in action.

The judge plays an important role in sorting out the evidence presented. You must appear credible and honest. The judge will ask questions and clarify information. S/he will not tolerate long winded diatribes, name calling or theatrics. Only hard evidence will be considered. The burden of proof is always on the plaintiff.

The goal is to reach a decision based on the information presented in court. Most landlord vs. tenant cases take fifteen to thirty minutes to complete.

Notes on courtroom behavior

- Have *all* of your records with you and organized so you can present them to the judge when needed. This will include a copy of the lease, copy of demand for possession and other notices, letter for "cure" and termination of lease, payment record and receipts, all correspondence between landlord and tenant, record of any monies deposited into the registry of the court, receipts for cleaning supplies and damage repairs, photographs of the property damage and anything else you feel pertinent to the case.
- Dress neatly and conservatively. Please no loud or ostentatious outfits and leave the gold watch and other obvious jewelry at home. You want to present yourself as the humble, hardworking landlord that you are.
- Speak loudly and clearly enough to be heard. Answer only the questions asked. Do not vent your personal feelings. Give all *pertinent* information.
- Address the judge as "your honor".
- Do not approach the judge. Give all papers and evidence to the clerk and s/he will pass things to the judge.
- Do not interrupt your opponent. Wait your turn; the judge will hear both sides of the case.

- Resist any baiting on the part of the tenant. Judges are human and will be watching your behavior. Present yourself calmly and maintain your dignity at all times.

Witnesses

While you will be the most important witness it may be helpful or necessary to have the testimony of another person. If you know someone who has *personal knowledge* of or documents supporting the facts on which your case is based and is willing to testify on your behalf ask them to come to court with you.

The court frowns on coaching a witness but acknowledges the need to discuss the case with the witness. Pre-trial preparation includes a through discussion of the facts of the case, the specific involvement of the witness and the possible questions the opposing side could ask.

Do not attempt to skew the evidence or encourage the witness to make false claims. It is illegal. A witness who lies under oath can be charged with perjury. Most likely the opposing side will detect any inconsistencies and discredit you and your witness.

If faced with a witness who does not want to testify, carefully weigh the benefit of any hostile testimony. If the witness can provide compelling evidence, regardless of his/her attitude, it may be necessary to *subpoena* the unwilling witness. A subpoena is a court order demanding the witness appear in court to testify.

In a case I observed regarding harassment by a tenant's children, the witnesses were afraid to testify willingly. The court issued subpoenas and each witness stated that her/his presence in the court room was not voluntary because s/he feared retaliation. The testimony was very effective and the landlord won possession of her property even though she had "unwilling" witnesses.

The eviction

After the writ of possession has been issued by the court it is sent to the marshal, constable or sheriff who will then contact the landlord or the eviction service to schedule the time and date of the eviction. Contact the marshal, constable or sheriff in your county to learn the exact procedure, as it varies slightly from county to county.

The landlord must pay for the eviction and provide the labor. A fee of $20.00 for *observing* the removal is payable to the marshal, sheriff or constable. You then hire your own help to physically move the furniture and other personal belongings out of the unit.

If your eviction crew should damage anything during the eviction, you can be held responsible for repair or replacement of the damaged goods. Try to find an eviction service that is insured. The eviction service will have your interests in mind and execute the writ of possession quickly. Fees vary and usually begin around $60.00 per thirty minutes.

I advise changing the locks *after* the tenant and the tenant's personal property has been removed. You can imagine the destruction that a very angry and recently evicted tenant could cause. Make sure *everything* has been removed as the tenant may try to break down the door to get to his/her belongings.

Needless to say, the eviction can be a highly charged situation. You have won your right to possession of the premises so don't rub it in. If you cannot resist taunting the tenant, stay away. This type of behavior will cause more hard feelings and may cause the evicted tenant to seek revenge.

The marshal does not have to be present. If you think there might be some danger it is advised to have some law enforcement official on site during the eviction.

Once the tenant is out, you must make a move out inspection. Inspect the dwelling and document all deficiencies on the move in/move out inspection form.

Run all water faucets and flush all toilets to make sure they have not been intentionally blocked or stopped up. Many eviction specialists tell me that a favorite mode of destruction is flooding. Departing tenants stop up all the sinks, toilets and tubs and turn the water on full force. You know how devastating water damage can be.

After obtaining a writ of possession (as a precaution), have the water bureau disconnect the water on the day the marshal is scheduled to supervise the eviction, and not before. You could use a water key to turn off the water but the tenant might also posses one. If notified in advance, the city will uncouple the pipes. There is a fee, but it is a small price to pay to protect your property from a tenant's revenge.

Have the move in/move out form ready for the tenant on the third day after the unit is vacated, as provided by Georgia law. Calculate charges and repair costs fairly. Any security deposit money must be handled as if the tenant voluntarily moved out upon the expiration of the lease. The dispossessory proceeding does not cancel the move out inspection or the prompt return of any funds.

If you find damage in excess of the security deposit funds you must decide if you want to seek additional compensation for the repairs. You can institute a small claim proceeding in Magistrate Court if your claim is less than $5,000.00.

Illegal eviction practices

You will find delinquent tenants the most frustrating people on earth. However, do not attempt any "do it yourself" eviction method. **Self help eviction is illegal in Georgia.** If you try this, you could be fined or even jailed. Think about it. You are in jail while your tenant still lives in your place rent free.

Although it may seem perfectly reasonable to throw your non-paying or destructive tenant out of your property, it is illegal in the eyes of Georgia law and you may leave yourself open to a costly lawsuit.

These are the things you, as a landlord, cannot do to evict your tenant:
- Remove doors and windows so the place is uninhabitable.
- Lock tenant out or change locks without notice.
- Turn off gas, electricity or water.
- Throw tenant and possessions into the street.
- Threaten bodily harm.

- Disturb the peace, or cause or permit a nuisance on the premises.
- Physically interfere with the tenant's right to possession of the rented property.
- Fail to make a necessary repair.

Chances are you will want to do all of these. Please restrain yourself and have your day in court.

Stay on top of it and do not let the tenant get behind in the rent, effect any breach or hold over. The moment the rent is past due or the lease is breached, begin the process of dispossessing your tenant.

Appeals

In a dispossessory action any ruling by the court may be appealed. Schedule your tenant's eviction as soon as it is legally possible since any notice of appeal will delay the eviction. You want the tenant out before s/he has a chance to appeal.

If your tenant appeals the judgment, you should immediately file a Motion to Compel Payment of Rent into Court Pending Appeal. Once again, the clerk will assist you through this process. If the tenant then fails to pay rent into the registry of the court as ordered you may file for an immediate writ of possession and proceed with the eviction—even if the case is on appeal. It will be up to you to determine whether or not the payments have been made as ordered by the court.

When to hire an attorney

- Anytime you experience fear of the legal process.
- If you have attempted any illegal remedy to force your tenant out.
- If you discover that all of your tenants have organized against you.
- If your tenant has a lawyer and has filed a written answer to your summons.
- If your tenant is a lawyer.

If you need a lawyer's help, do not hesitate to seek it at any stage of the dispossessory process. However, just because your tenant hires a lawyer doesn't mean that you have to. If you are thoroughly versed in the dispossessory process and have made every effort to follow the required procedures, you may prefer to act as your own attorney. In many cases landlords have more experience than lawyers.

When choosing a lawyer, ask how long s/he has been in practice, what schools s/he attended, what experience s/he has had in similar matters and what, if any, complaints have been filed against him or her. Make sure the lawyer you choose is skilled in handling tenant/landlord cases. Ask how many landlords s/he has represented. Please do not allow your case to be lost because you have hired an attorney who is not familiar with tenant/landlord law.

You will probably be quite harried and frustrated by this point. Nonetheless, do not make ridiculous demands on the lawyer you have hired. Lawyers' biggest complaint about landlords is their unrealistic expectations and demands. Nothing short of the tenant's immediate removal will satisfy an angry landlord, yet lawyers are subject to the same legal process that binds the landlord. A lawyer cannot remove your tenant at will, nor can s/he file papers on a Saturday.

Remember that your lawyer has many clients and cannot drop everything to handle your case. On the other hand, you are entitled to timely representation. If your lawyer is too busy for you, find another one.

When you meet with your lawyer, prepare as carefully as you would to go to court. Take a copy of you lease agreement, payment records, copies of any complaint notices and any other information you might have regarding this tenant. If you need witnesses to substantiate any claims, have their names and addresses so they can be called to appear in court and testify in your behalf.

You may want to vent your personal feelings when you talk to your lawyer. Don't. Present your problem calmly. Be clear and concise. Chances are s/he has heard it before and just wants the facts. Call your therapist for a special ninety minute session to vent your "tenant anger" or spend a few hours in a batting cage. Your lawyer can only provide legal remedies. Listen to your options, ask questions and decide on a course of action. Then, let your lawyer do his/her job.

Fees should be discussed during the first consultation. This initial meeting will cost $75.00 to $150.00. After that, fees will accrue according to how much work is done. Expect to pay $25.00 for each **Strict Compliance** and **Demand** letter. In addition, be prepared to pay service, court appearance and filing fees. Make sure you understand the extent of your financial obligations by discussing all possible fees in advance. You don't want to be unpleasantly surprised when you get the bill.

If you decide to use a lawyer referral service, do the same detailed investigation of the referral agency's credentials that you did on your prospective tenant, credit reporting service or eviction service. Ask lots of questions. Find out how long they have been in business, get a reference from someone who has used their service, get the names of several attorneys who use the service and call them. Do not use any referral services that require a payment from you for an attorney's name.

Here are a few sources to help you find an attorney:

Atlanta Bar Association Referral Service	404-521-0777
Cobb County Bar Association	404-424-7149
DeKalb Bar Association	404-373-2580
Savannah Bar Association	912-356-9272
State Bar of Georgia:	
For listings in other cities	404-527-8700

In addition, *Martindale-Hubbell Law Directory* is published annually by Reed Publishing. This book gives a brief description of the listed attorney's practice and each attorney is rated by his/her colleagues. You may find it in your public library, any law school library or any other legal library in your area. Many attorneys keep a copy in their office.

---

[1] This gives the tenant five days to pay up or get out. On the sixth day file a dispossessory affidavit.

CHAPTER SIX

Other Remedies

How to collect past due rent or fees for damages

Short of pursuing a dispossesion, these are the other legal remedies for collecting past due rent or fees for damages:

- Distraint Proceeding
- Civil Action

Distraint proceeding

Distraint is the right of the landlord to seize the tenant's property to satisfy the rental obligation. If the rent is past due or your tenant is seeking to remove his property from the premises you can begin distraint proceedings. (Note: "Distress" is another term that is sometimes used in place of "distraint". The two terms are interchangable.) The landlord is issued a *lien,* which is a claim, encumbrance or charge on property for payment of some debt, on the tenant's *leviable property* (property that has some value and is not exempt from seizure).

This option is practical only if the tenant has valuable and unencumbered property. "Valuable" means that you can realize enough cash from the sale of the property to satisfy the past due rent amount. "Unencumbered" means that the property is free of previous liens and not protected by homestead exemption. You cannot seize property that is used professionally by the tenant. For example, a workman's tools are exempt as is a musician's piano. It is up to the landlord to prove ownership.

Distraint proceedings are available to the landlord but not terribly practical. This law's requirements render it all but useless for the payment of past due rent.

The landlord is required to notify the tenant of an impending distraint order, usually by writing a letter giving the tenant ten days to pay up or face legal proceedings. As one can imagine, this gives the tenant ample time to conceal or remove his/her property before the landlord can seize it.

The property you intend to seize must have a value equal to the rent you are owed to be of any benefit to you. Unless the tenant has very high quality furnishings or an incredible art collection you won't get much benefit from this.

To file a distraint:

1. You must be able to prove a tenant-landlord relationship exists.
2. The rent must be past due or tenant must be seeking to remove his leviable property.
3. The tenant must reside in or have property in the county where you file the distraint.

Your lease will establish the tenant-landlord relationship and also indicate when rent is past due. As in any legal proceeding, make sure you can prove your case and have thorough documentation for all claims. If you lose your distraint action, the tenant is entitled to damages caused by your wrongful conduct.

If your situation meets these conditions, go to the courthouse in the county where the tenant's property is located and file a Distraint (or Distress) Affidavit. Again, the court will provide pre-printed forms. State that the tenant is attempting to remove his/her property from the premises or that rent is past due. You do not have to demand rental payment or possession in this proceeding.

Once the tenant has been served the summons s/he cannot "transfer, convey, remove or conceal his property".

If the tenant fails to answer the summons within seven days s/he is in default and the landlord is awarded a distraint warrant and a default judgment for all rents due. Be prepared to provide proper evidence for how much rent is due. Your lease agreement is best, but rental payment receipts that show the amount paid will do. A tenant in default may request an additional thirty days to answer.

Once again the tenant is given a great deal of leeway when filing his/her answer. Any allegation that s/he denies will be heard and ruled on by the court. If allegations are not denied they are deemed admitted. The tenant is allowed to remain in possession of the premises and his/her property pending the final outcome of the trial if s/he pays rental payments into the registry of the court.

When the tenant files an answer s/he is required to pay to the registry of the court any rent which accrued prior to the issue of the summons. However, if s/he denies owing any back rent, s/he cannot be forced to pay it into the court's registry. The tenant *must* pay into the registry of the court any rent that accrues after the summons has been issued. Again, be prepared to present a copy of your lease or the last rent payment to prove how much rent is due. Rather than pay rent into the registry, the tenant may opt to post a surety bond for an amount that is equal to or greater than the amount alleged in your affidavit.

If the tenant fails to either pay rent into the registry or to post a surety bond s/he cannot stay in possession of the property pending the trial. It is your responsibility to notify the court of this. The property is now subject to seizure to be held for *levy* (the legal method of seizing property or cash for an unpaid debt) and sale. After you notify the court of the tenant's failure to pay or post bond, ask for a court order granting you permission to seize the tenant's property.

The tenant is entitled to pay all rents allegedly owed and the cost of the distraint warrant within seven days of being served the warrant. This is a complete defense and closes the case. This option is not limited to one time in twelve months as is the case in a dispossessory proceeding. Each time you file a distraint proceeding the tenant can pay past due rent and the cost of the warrant to satisfy your claim against him/her.

If your tenant has answered, but the answer is unacceptable to the court and the court has ruled in your favor then you have won the right to levy and sell the tenant's furniture. Now the real work begins.

The levied goods, your tenant's furniture, will be moved to and stored in a bonded warehouse where they will await advertisement and sale. You are responsible for the cost of moving and storage. It is possible to store the seized furniture on your premises if you do not desire their immediate use. Most landlords prefer to get the stuff out and re-rent the unit.

Expenses such as marshal's fees, auctioneer's fees, storage, moving and advertising fees will be deducted from the proceeds of the sale. Whatever is left is what you collect from your distraint action.

A landlord may request a re-levy to satisfy any balance due but s/he must present documents that indicate the amount of the distraint warrant, the amount realized by the levy and sale of the goods and the difference between those amounts.

You can see why few landlords resort to attaching the furniture. Distraint is too costly.

Civil action

If a tenant owes you money for unpaid rent, damages over the security deposit or other breaches of the lease you can bring a small claims suit in Magistrate Court provided your claim does not exceed $5,000.00 and the statute of limitations has not run out. The statute of limitations for collecting damages to rental property and unpaid rent is four years. If you wait two or three years before filing, the judge may wonder why it took you so long and ask why you waited.

Magistrate Court is a user friendly court. The Magistrate Court system in Georgia is set up for the express purpose of hearing cases presented by ordinary citizens. You may have a lawyer present if you wish but you don't have to.

First determine if you have a case against your tenant. Take a moment to answer the following questions:

1. What happened?
2. Who caused the problem? The person sued must be the person who is legally responsible for your loss.
3. Is the tenant wrong (i.e. liable)?
4. Is money due?
5. How much money is due?
6. Has the statute of limitations run out?
7. What proof do you have?

The best type of case for small claims court is one where the dispute is specific, can be documented and can be resolved by a cash settlement.

There are three types of liability:

1. Negligence (i.e. the tenant acted irresponsibly).
2. Intentionally or willfully causing damage or harm.
3. Breach of contract (i.e. the tenant failed to abide by the terms of the lease).

If the tenant failed to exercise "reasonable care" s/he is negligent and is therefore responsible for damages caused by his/her careless actions. For example, if the tenant took an axe to the walls and doors of the rental unit it is reasonably safe to say the tenant intentionally or willfully caused damage.

If a valid contract, such as a lease agreement exists, and you can show that the contract has been broken and that as a result of the breach you have suffered a loss, you may then establish liability due to breach of contract.

If the tenant has already vacated the property an eviction proceeding is *not* an alternative to a civil action. When a tenant skips out, bringing an action for rent is your only means of getting past due rent. A copy of the lease and your payment records are necessary to prove how much rent is past due.

In your suit for unpaid rent you can also ask for any other claims you may have against the tenant such as damages, payment for removal of inoperable vehicles left on the premises or removal and storage of personal belongings. This is called a *joinder*. You can join the claims if the court has the jurisdiction to do so.

You may also use this option if the damages exceed the security deposit paid. You must provide estimates and receipts for work done to restore your unit to its original condition, wear and tear excepted. Make sure you provide clearly documented receipts. Photographs of the damage are quite helpful.

Notice must be given before you start the civil suit. Write a letter to the tenant stating what was done wrongly, what is owed and when it should be paid. Your notice will give the tenant ten days to pay or face legal action.

If your lease contains a mutual provision for attorney fees, you must give notice that this obligation will be enforced and the prevailing party will be entitled to collect attorney's fees. (Georgia law allows both the landlord and the tenant to ask for attorney's fees in matters arising from the lease of a dwelling.) You can notify the tenant of your intention to seek attorney's fees either in the notice given prior to instituting the suit, in the suit itself or up until ten days prior to judgment on the suit.

A small claims action is filed in a manner similar to the dispossessory proceeding. Pre-printed forms are available in the Clerk's Office and the clerk of the court can help you fill out the forms properly. Some offices have examples posted on the bulletin board.

Fill out the affidavit, swear to it and pay the filing fee. A summons is issued by the court and served by the marshall, constable or sheriff. The defendant, your tenant, has thirty days to answer.

If the tenant fails to answer s/he is in default and you will be awarded a judgment for the amount alleged in your affidavit. Have your evidence on hand just in case you need it.

If the tenant answers, a trial date is set and you must appear to present your case to the judge. Prepare as carefully for small claims court as you would for a dispossessory hearing. You must appear in court on the appointed day to present your side even if the defendant does not show up.

Bring accurate documents that will show what damage has been done and how much it cost to repair or replace the damaged items. In tenant vs. landlord matters, always bring a copy of your lease to court. When possible have photographs of any damage.

Quite often the other side will make a settlement offer. This offer is generally less than the amount you claimed in the law suit. It is up to you to decide whether or not the offer is fair and whether you will accept it.

If you decide to accept the settlement offer, do not dismiss your case until you have full payment. The offer could be a ploy by the tenant to get you to drop the case. Make sure you protect yourself and get payment in cash or by money order before notifying the court that you have settled the case.

Demand a written settlement agreement between yourself and the defendant.

Sample settlement agreement:

It is agreed by _Margaret Manager, plaintiff_ and _Tammy Tenant_, _defendant_, in Case Number_____ filed in_____County that the above action will be settled for the amount of $_____.

This sum was received in full by _Margaret Manager_ from _Tammy Tenant_ on _date_.

Plaintiff, Margaret Manager, will notify the court and dismiss the case.

If the defendant defaults on this agreement, the plaintiff shall have the right to initiate court action to collect both the above sum and the additional cost of collection including court costs and attorneys' fees.

_____
Plaintiff   Date

_____
Defendant   Date

Winning the case is not the same as having cash in your bank account. If the judge rules in your favor and awards the damages claimed it is up to you to collect the judgment. The judge is not responsible for collecting the money due and you are not given cash on the spot to satisfy the judgment.

How to collect money judgments awarded by the court
- Record a *writ of fieri facias (fi. fa.)*
- Levy the tenant's bank account or property
- Garnish the tenant's wages
- Hire a collection agency

Since you had to get a judgment from the court it is pretty clear that the defendant has no intention of paying you. However, you must make one last request for payment in writing before taking any other action.

Next, record the judgment on the General Execution Document, which is a listing of court rulings made against the defendant. Then file a writ of fieri facias (also known as a fi. fa.) in the Clerk's Office. This writ places a lien on any property of the defendant for seven years. You can renew it for as long as your judgment remains uncollected.

If your tenant does not currently own any property do not despair. When the tenant tries to purchase or inherits property this judgment will show up and the tenant will have to settle his/her obligation to you before s/he can complete any transaction related to the new property. Credit reporting agencies read the court records to find out if any judgements exist against someone so, by filing the writ and having the judgment recorded, you have blemished the tenant's credit report.

When you execute a levy, a marshal or sheriff removes property, jewelry, funds from bank accounts, business assets, cash from the till or other personal possessions belonging to the defendant that will satisfy the amount of your judgement. The marshal can actually remove watches, diamond rings, stereo equipment, televisions, etc. from the defendant's residence or person. Be careful to take only items that belong to the defendant. Certain items such as tools required to perform one's trade (a musician's guitar, a carpenter's toolbox, etc.) are exempt from a levy.

If you know where the defendant banks and his/her account number you may have the marshal levy the account for enough funds to satify your judgement. It is best to wait until there are funds adequate to satisfy the amount of your judgment in the account, but it is easy to open and close bank accounts so you will need to move as quickly as possible in order to seize the money due to you.

To *garnish* is to deduct money from the defendant's income, usually wages or commissions, for payment of a debt. You cannot garnish social security, V.A. benefits or welfare payments. The court will notify your ex-tenant's employer that his/her wages are to be garnished. This means the employer is required to deduct ten to twenty-five percent of the debtor's paycheck each week and send that amount to you until the debt is satisfied. As wages are paid on a regular basis and there is little that can be done to prevent you from garnishing them, this method of collection is your best bet.

Once again you will find yourself in the Clerk's Office, this time to file an Affidavit for Garnishment. The defendant's employer will be contacted and ordered to deduct a certain percentage of the debtor's wages.

If neither the defendant's employer, bank account nor property is located in the county where you obtained your judgment you must go to the county where the employer, bank account or property is located to try and collect on it. It's the same procedure, just a different courthouse.

If you are not certain of the existence or location of the tenant's assets, you can request an examination of assets.

At this point however, you may be too fed up to proceed any further. Consider hiring a collection agency instead. Most collection agencies work on a contingency basis. That is, they are paid a set percentage of the amount collected. In the case of collecting judgments for rent the contingency fee is thirty to fifty percent. This means that the collection agency will keep thirty to fifty percent of the money collected on your judgment.

However, a claim from a collection agency will show up on the tenant's credit report. Using a collection agency known for its work in the area of landlord-tenant collections will alert the next unsuspecting landlord.

To find a good collection agency, use the guidelines supplied in chapter seven for evaulating credit reporting services.

CHAPTER SEVEN

Service Agencies for Landlords

Credit reporting services

You may decide to use a credit reporting agency to verify the information provided by a prospective tenant. I have found companies with very reasonable fees and quick turn around times. Their resources and experience can be quite beneficial.

You will find numerous agencies listed in the Yellow Pages™ under "Credit Reporting Agencies." Look over the listings to get some idea of the number of resources available to you.

You can immediately discard the agencies whose services are limited to mortgage reports and employment checks. These companies cannot offer you the level of service needed to establish the credibility of your rental applicant.

Plan to spend a few hours interviewing different agencies since you need to develop a good working relationship with your credit reporting service. You will rely heavily upon the information they report to you. Selecting an agency who supplies you with incomplete information could cause you to make a regrettable decision.

The idea behind obtaining credit, employment and rental histories is to limit your chances of renting to an undesirable tenant. It makes your life much easier if you can avoid tenants who skip out, don't pay the rent on time or are veterans of the dispossessory wars. The bottom line is that you want to find good tenants who pay their rent on time.

Try to get a feel for the agency's attitude. You want to find someone with a real zeal for this type of work—someone who enjoys looking into the affairs of others. In addition, you want hard facts not hearsay. There are dedicated professionals in this business and it is possible to locate a reputable agency.

A simple retail credit report will not provide enough information for you to decide whether or not to rent to an applicant. Collect credit, employment and rental histories. An accurate rental history is much more valuable to a landlord than a retail credit history since retail credit reports do not show the prospective tenant's rental payment patterns, treatment of rental property or other specifics. On the other hand, a rental history will tell you if there have been any noise complaints or other problems with the tenant and the condition in which s/he left past apartments in addition to his/her payment history.

You want an agency that will thoroughly investigate, not merely confirm, the information your rental applicant has given. This requires some knowledge of the area, experience in spotting false information, and expertise in obtaining rental histories.

Be sure to ask the following questions while interviewing credit reporting agencies:

- *What kind of experience do you have?* Require at least five to ten years experience in assisting residential property managers. Ask how long they have been in business and how long the have been doing property management reports for landlords. An agency with twenty years experience in credit checking is not adequate for your needs. If this agency does not usually serve landlords or property managers, they don't know what to look for.
- *What services do you offer?* Let *them* tell you what they do. If they don't mention thorough previous residence checks this is not the agency for you.
- *What are your fees?* There should be no hesitation about quoting fees over the phone. Generally fees of $15.00 to $30.00 per report are within range. Some agencies may require a membership fee, which should be in the range of $20.00 to $50.00.
- *What is your turn-around time?* This is credit reporting language for "When will I get my report?" The agency should be able to report back to you within 24 to 48 hours.

  NOTE: Don't let prospective tenants try to rush you on the credit report in order to move in more quickly. Be suspicious of applicants who want a report in less time than this. They probably have something to hide. Companies frown on requests for rush jobs because they feel they won't have enough time to get a complete report on the applicant.
- *Do you operate under the standards set by the Fair Credit Reporting Act?* Be suspicious of long convoluted responses to this question. The Fair Credit Reporting Act is a federal law. Failure to comply with it can result in stiff fines. You do not want to get involved with some shyster who breaks the law.

Here's the low-down on the three biggest credit bureaus:

- **Equifax:** 800-685-1111, Atlanta Sales: 404-256-4100, fax line: 404-612-3150. It took them almost a month to respond to my request for information. The membership fee is $150.00 and they require a monthly minimum fee of $40.00. The sales office suggested that a small landlord would do better with a smaller credit reporting agency as most small agencies access Equifax for credit data. The salesperson referred me to four smaller agencies in the Atlanta area.
- **Trans Union:** 312-408-0919, Sales: 312-408-1077, fax line: 312-347-5774. Trans Union provides single property management reports. Their fees are competitive and they responded quickly to my request. Check your Yellow Pages™ for a local number. However, with this option, you lose the benefit of a local agency's knowledge of the area.

- **TRW:** 800-275-4879. TRW is not interested in serving small or casual landlords. They cater to big businesses. The membership fee of $500.00 and monthly minimum fee of $50.00 was enough to discourage me.

Utilizing a smaller, local agency has many advantages. Their familiarity with the local area is important because most tenants do not stray too far. It is easier for a local person to spot a trend and track the tenant's behavior.

The landlord is required to tell the prospective tenant that his/her credit is being investigated. In addition you must obtain his/her written consent. Make sure your rental application contains the following language in some form:

"I authorize landlord or his /her agent to confirm the information listed in this application, to communicate with my employer, creditors and any credit reporting agency, and to procure such other information as landlord or agent may require to evaluate this application." Do not forget to have the tenant sign the rental application giving you permission to obtain a background report.

Do not expect the credit reporting agency to select your tenants for you. This is your job. You must decide to whom you will rent your dwelling based on their personal appearance, their credit, employment and rental histories and any other information you have managed to gather in interviews and from personal visits.

If you reject an applicant based on the information obtained from a credit report you are not obliged to debate the validity of the information with the tenant. You are required, by law, to give the rental applicant the name, address and phone number of the credit reporting service that supplied the report to you. This matter is now between the rental applicant and the credit reporting agency. You stay out of it!

Do not obtain credit reports on your friends, enemies or associates. You may request reports only for a "permissible purpose": in connection with a rental or retail transaction, for employment purposes or in connection with a legitimate business transaction. If you obtain a consumer credit report under false pretenses you can face a fine of up to $5,000 or up to one year of imprisonment, or both. It's not a good idea to abuse your credit reporting agency's patience with frivolous requests.

You are required to hold in strict confidence all information received from any credit reporting service. You can be sued for damages and legal fees if you are not diligent in protecting the rental applicant's privacy. Do not be tempted to share any applicant or tenant's credit information with others.

The Fair Credit Reporting Act was instituted to insure that credit reporting agencies exercise their responsibilities with fairness, impartiality and respect for a consumer's right to privacy. Be sure to conduct yourself in a manner consistent with these goals.

Obligation to provide rental histories

As a landlord you will be called upon to provide rental histories on your tenants. Do not use this as an opportunity to get back at a tenant who rubbed you the wrong way. If s/he paid the rent on time and left your unit undamaged you must report this. On the other hand, if you had to institute dispossessory proceedings against this tenant do not hesitate to provide this information. Remember how important an accurate rental history is to you when considering a rental application.

Eviction services

This may be a hard service to locate. The Yellow Pages™ contain an "Eviction Service" heading. It's a start. Spending time around the Marshal's Office will give you an opportunity to meet people who own or operate eviction service companies.

Call large apartment complexes and ask the property managers. Ask which company they use, how their service is and how much they charge. Specify that you are looking for an agency that will actually remove property and goods from your unit(s), since some agencies merely handle the dispossessory process.

One word of caution: If an agency offers credit reporting as well as dispossessory, collection and eviction services, take some time to investigate. If this agency is less than ethical it may give you bad or limited information on the tenant's initial credit/employment history because it will also benefit from assisting you with the subsequent eviction. Landlord be aware!

Since the marshal merely supervises the eviction, the landlord must provide the labor. Fees usually range from $120.00 to $130.00 per hour. Eviction agencies usually quote prices per *half* hour so they don't sound so high. When you hear $60.00 to $65.00 check if it is for thirty minutes or one hour.

Many eviction services will handle all of the dispossessory paper work and warrant filing for you. The fees range from $17.00 to $25.00 plus court costs for filing the affidavit and warrant.

The landlord can be held liable for any damage to the property resulting from its removal. Question the eviction agency about the crew and its experience. You do not want some gorilla crew tossing things over the balcony. Select an agency that is bonded or carries some type of liability insurance. You will have to specifically ask if the eviction personnel are insured or bonded. Get confirmation of such in writing.

Apartment owners associations

To locate the apartment owners association in your area you can ask large apartment complexes, look them up in the phone book or ask any of the credit reporting services you have interviewed.

The associations usually have the name of the town or county where they are located in their business name. For instance, the name of the association in Atlanta, Georgia is the Atlanta Apartment Association. Contact the National Apartment Association at 202·842-4050 and ask for the name and phone number of the apartment association in your area.

These associations are quite helpful. As a member you will have access to pre-printed forms for rental applications, security deposit inspections, lease agreements, smoke detector inspections, etc. The association also publishes an extensive service guide.

Most apartment associations conduct training sessions presented by skilled professionals who cover topics ranging from property management to recapturing refrigerant.

The companies listed in the association's service guide are members. While the association does not endorse these companies, this listing serves as a good initial screening process for you. Most are reputable since dishonest companies will not pay the fees nor provide the information necessary for membership in the apartment owner's association.

Publications to further assist landlords

Questions Frequently Asked by Tenants and Landlords
Published by: Georgia Housing & Finance Authority
60 Executive Parkway South, Atlanta, GA 30329
Georgia attorneys have provided the material for this booklet, which is written in a question and answer format for landlords and tenants. Write for a free copy.

Landlord Tenant Law Bulletin
Published by: Ouinlan Publishing Company
23 Drydock Avenue, Boston, MA 02210-2387
Reviews landlord-tenant legal proceedings nationwide in an easy-to-read synopsis form. Write for a free copy and index.

Professional Apartment Management
Published by: Brownstone Publishers, Inc.
304 Park Avenue South, NY, NY 10010-4302
A monthly publication that presents a legal review, advertising and promotion ideas for getting and keeping tenants and current issues relevant to landlords such as insurance, wear and tear and discrimination. Write for sample issue.

Additional Resources
— Georgia Association of Real Estate Investors
— Georgia Association of Realtors
— Building Owners and Managers Association of Georgia

INDEX

A

abandon the property, 7, 24, 28
administrative fee, 33
advance rent, 39
Affidavit for Garnishment, 70
altering the premises, 27
answer the summons, 52-53, 66
apartment owners associations, 76
appeals, 61
application fee, 3, 33, 39
Atlanta Apartment Association, 76
Atlanta Bar Association
    Referral Service, 62
attorney fees, 68
authorization, 4

B

background check, 3
bank references, 3
bankruptcy, 56
breach, 13, 16, 18-19, 22, 26-27, 29, 45-46, 51, 61
breach of the lease, 26, 31, 43, 67-68
burden of proof, 56, 58

C

canceling the lease, 44
cash, 2, 12, 21, 31, 33-34, 47, 65-66, 68-70
cashier's check, 2, 12, 21, 31, 33-34
changing locks, 28
city/county codes, 27
civil action, 65, 67-68
cleaning fees, 31-33, 37, 39
cleanliness, 7
clerk of the court, 53, 68
Cobb County Bar Association, 62
Code of Georgia, 11, 43
collect money judgments, 69-71
collection agencies, 7, 71
commercial rentals, 11
condo association, 28
condominium instruments, rules and
    regulations, 19, 28
constructive eviction, 56
cooling off period, 8
courtroom etiquette, 57-58
credit cards, 21
credit check, 5, 74
credit report, 2, 3, 5, 70-71, 73-75
credit reporting agencies, 4, 5, 62, 70-71, 73-76
cure of breach, 26, 45, 47

D

damages, 12-14, 19, 22, 26, 31-32, 37- 39, 51, 54, 65, 66-69, 75
default, 16, 26, 28, 29, 53, 66, 69
defects in the premises, 26
defendant's answer, 53
DeKalb Bar Association, 62
delivery method, 49
demand for possession, 26, 45, 47-50, 58

demand for possession for failure to cure breach of the lease, 49
demand for possession for non-payment of rent, 47
demand for possession to a tenant holding over, 48
discrimination, 6, 8, 77
discussion of the facts, 59
dispossessory, 1, 43, 48, 50-51
dispossessory affidavit, 45, 49, 58, 62
dispossessory clerk, 51
dispossessory index, 3, 8
dispossessory proceeding, 16, 23-24, 26-27, 34, 43-44, 49-50, 52-53, 55, 60
dispossessory warrant, 50, 52, 54, 55, 56
distraint, 65, 66
distraint (or distress) affidavit, 66
distraint proceedings, 65
distraint warrant, 66, 67
do it yourself eviction, 60

E

employment references, 3, 4
Equifax, 74
escrow, 13, 31, 57
estimation of damage, 23
eviction, 1, 43, 53-54, 59, 60
eviction agencies, 59, 76
eviction service, 7, 59, 62, 76
evidence, 27, 44, 51, 56, 57-59, 66, 69
ex-tenant's employer, 70
excessive late fees, 22

F

failure to surrender the premises, 43
Fair Credit Reporting Act, 74-75
false claims, 44, 52, 59
familial status, 2, 7-8
fee list, 32
filing fee, 44, 51-52, 62, 68
final inspection, 39
fire hazard, 3, 14, 25
first month's rent, 2, 31, 33

G

garnish, 70
general rules and regulations, 28
Georgia Code Annotated, Title 61, 11
Georgia law, 11, 22, 23, 24, 32, 37, 38, 39, 43, 53, 54, 60, 68
Georgia Security Deposit Act, 31

H

handicap, 2, 8
hold over, 15, 25, 61
housing authority, 11
how to collect past due rent, 65

I

illegal eviction, 60
impending distraint, 65
income stability, 5, 6
inspection of the property, 22
intention to enter notice, 15
interest earning account, 31, 37-39
interviewing credit reporting agencies, 73-74

J

joinder, 68

K

key deposit, 33, 34

L

landlord has not made repairs, 27, 32, 55
Landlord Tenant Law Bulletin, 77
landlord's inspection, 23, 38
late fees, 12-13, 22, 31, 37, 39, 44, 54
late rental payments, 22, 45
lease, 2, 11-12, 14, 20-21, 26, 38, 57, 66

lease agreement, 8, 11, 16, 20-24, 26, 32, 37, 43-45, 48-49, 51, 55, 62, 68, 77
lease term, 13, 15, 19
legal eviction, 43
legal action, 25
legal fees, 26, 39, 75
legal notices, 23
legal remedies, 27, 62, 65
legally ejected, 4, 24, 44
letter demanding cure for breach of lease, 46
leviable property, 65-67
levy, 66, 67, 70
lien, 65, 70

M

Magistrate or State Court, 1, 51, 57, 60, 67
marital status, 4
Martindale-Hubbell Law Directory, 62
Military personnel, 24
money judgment, 53
money order, 2, 12, 21, 31, 33-34, 56, 69
money to cover the deposit and rent, 2
mortgagees' rights, 17, 28
motion, 61
move in inspection, 32
move out inspection, 32, 38, 60
move out procedure, 13, 19, 28, 31, 37

N

nail and mail, 53
National Apartment Association, 76
negligence, 13, 15, 26-27, 32, 68
no smoking policy, 3, 6
non-payment of rent, 29, 43, 45, 48, 50, 56
non-refundable cleaning fee, 13, 23
non-refundable fees, 33, 39
notice, 12, 14, 17, 19, 21, 24, 25, 37, 39, 49, 55

notice of any rent increase, 21
notice of intention to enter, 58
notice of intention to vacate, 37
notice of termination, 15
notification of move out, 37
number of occupants, 2, 6, 14, 25

O

observation day, 58
ordinances, 27

P

pass keys, 28
payment method, 12, 17
personal references, 7
pets, 3, 6, 15, 26
photographs, 58, 68, 69
plaintiff prays or demands, 51
possession, 12-13, 15-16, 21, 24-25, 34, 51
pre-qualification, 1
pre-trial, 57, 59
preliminary checkpoints, 2
presenting your case, 57
previous landlord, 2, 3, 5, 6
pro se, 57
pro se litigants, 51
procedural error, 50
Professional Apartment Management, 77
property loss, 15, 26

Q

qualify all prospects, 1

R

reason for filing, 51
reasonable effort, 23, 40
receipt book, 56
refundable fees, 39
refunding deposits, 39
refusal of payment, 50

registry of the court, 57-58, 61, 66
rent, 1-7, 8, 12, 21
rent collector, 21
rent increases, 21
rental history, 33, 73, 76
rental/lease agreement, 29
repair and deduct, 55
repairs, 16, 27, 55
replacement fees, 32
request for verification of deposit, 2, 4
reserve funds, 33
residential rental agreement, 11
returned checks, 12, 22

S

Savannah Bar Association, 62
schedule of the fees charged, 32
Section Eight, 11, 43
security deposit, 3, 13, 22, 31, 33, 39
security deposit inspection, 32
security deposit refund, 13, 23
self help eviction, 60
settlement agreement, 69
settlement offer, 69
small claims, 53, 67-69
smoke detectors, 17
State Bar of Georgia, 62
statute of limitations, 67
storage, 18
strict compliance, 16, 29, 45-47, 62
sublease, 24
subletting, 14, 24
subpoena, 59
substitution for rent, 55
summary of move in fees, 23
surety bond, 13, 22, 31, 66
surrender and acceptance, 22, 38-39

T

tenancy at sufferance, 24-25, 43, 48
tenancy at will, 23-25, 43, 48
tenant abandons the unit, 16
tenant answers, 53

tenant at sufferance who is holding over, 45
tenant at will who is holding over, 45
tenant dissents, 38, 53
tenant holding over, 43, 49-50, 54
tenant tricks, 56
term, 20
termination notice, 16-18, 22-23, 31, 58
timely rental payment, 6
Trans Union, 74
TRW, 75
types of liability, 68

U

unauthorized decorating, 27
unauthorized person obtained access, 28
unencumbered property, 65
unused security deposit money, 22, 32
utilities, 4, 14, 21, 24, 37

V

vehicles, 3, 6, 18-19, 68
verify income, 4, 6
violation, 16, 18, 26, 44-46, 51

W

waterbeds, 3, 6, 18
wear and tear, 2, 13, 16, 19-20, 22, 25, 32, 38, 68, 77
when to hire an attorney, 61
witnesses, 57, 59, 62
writ of fieri facias, 70
writ of possession, 16, 28, 52-54, 59, 60-61

APPENDIX

Sample Forms and Letters

Date _____

Rental Application

PLEASE COMPLETE EACH BLANK

A non-refundable fee of $_____ is required for processing this application.
(If applicant is accepted as a resident, this application is to become part of the rental agreement)

Applicant's Name _____   Co-Applicant's Name _____

Date of Birth _____   Date of Birth _____

Social Security Number _____   Social Security Number _____

Marital Status _____   Marital Status _____

OTHER PERSONS TO RESIDE IN APARTMENT

Name	Relationship	Age		Name	Relationship	Age

1. _____   3. _____

2. _____   4. _____

RENTAL HISTORY

Present Address _____   Phone _____   How Long _____

Present Landlord _____   Phone _____   Rent $ _____

Immediate Previous Address _____   Phone _____   How Long _____

Previous Landlord _____   Phone _____   Rent $ _____

Next Previous Address _____   Phone _____   How Long _____

Next Previous Landlord _____   Phone _____   Rent $ _____

Have you ever been evicted from any leased premises? Yes ( ) No ( )

If Yes, Explain _____

Reason for leaving present address _____

EMPLOYMENT INFORMATION

Present Employer _____   Supervisor _____   Phone _____

Address _____ City _____ State _____ Zip _____   Monthly Income $ _____

Position _____   Date Employed _____

Previous Employer _____   Supervisor _____   Phone _____

Address _____ City _____ State _____ Zip _____   Monthly Income $ _____

Position _____   Date Employed _____

Reason for Leaving _____

Co-Applicant's Present Employer _____   Supervisor _____   Phone _____

Address _____ City _____ State _____ Zip _____   Monthly Income $ _____

Position _____   Date Employed _____

CREDIT HISTORY

BANK REFERENCE

Name of Institution   Address   Account Type and Number

1. _____
2. _____
3. _____

CHARGE ACCOUNTS/CREDIT CARDS

Name   Account Number

1. _____
2. _____
3. _____

CURRENT MONTHLY OBLIGATIONS (Car payment, bank loans, etc.)

Name   Type/Account Number   Monthly Payment

1. _____
2. _____
3. _____

PERSONAL REFERENCES

Name   Address   Phone

1. _____
2. _____
3. _____

AUTO

Make & Color   Year   Lic. Tag Number   State

1. _____
2. _____
3. _____

Applicant's Driver's License No. _____

State _____

Do you own a motorcycle, van, boat, trailer, truck or camper? _____

If so, specify _____

Co-Applicant's Driver's License No. _____

State _____

MISCELLANEOUS

Nearest Relative Not living With You and person to notify in emergencies:

Name   Address   Phone   Relationship

1. _____
2. _____

Are you subject to transfer? Yes ( ) No ( ) _____

Reason _____
_____

Do you smoke? Yes ( ) No ( )

Do you have a waterbed? Yes ( ) No ( )

Do you have a pet? Yes ( ) No ( )

If "Yes" please specify _____

Weight when full grown ___ lbs.

Do you have friends or relatives living in the complex? Yes ( ) No ( ) Name _____

I/we certify that the information given herein is complete, true and correct. Landlord or his/her agent is hereby expressly authorized to verify the accuracy and correctness of these statements, to communicate with my/our employer, previous landlords and creditors to obtain my credit, employment and rental histories and to procure such other information which Landlord or Agent may require to evaluate this application. Application must be signed by all adults who will occupy the unit before it can be considered by Landlord.

Applicant _____ Date _____

Co-Applicant _____ Date _____

Request for Verification of Deposit

(Company Name) _____
(Rental Address) _____
(City, State, Zip) _____

TO:

RE: __*(Print or type renter's name here)*__

Account # _____

Type _____

Date _____

I, _____*(Renter's signature here)*_____ , authorize you to verify this information and to supply the landlord identified above with information regarding my credit history with your depository.

Checking/Savings

| Account Number | Current Balance | Average Balance Previous Two Months |

1. _____
2. _____
3. _____

Bank Cards

Type & Account Number   Current Balance   Avg. Monthly payment

1. _____
2. _____
3. _____

Outstanding Loans

Loan Number   Date of Loan   Amount   Current Balance   Monthly Payment

1. _____
2. _____
3. _____

If any late payments on any outstanding loans please give dates: _____
_____

_____   _____   _____
Signature of Depository   Title   Date

This form is to be transmitted directly to the Landlord and is not to be transmitted through the applicant or any other party.

Employment Verification

Name of Employer _____

Address _____

City _____ State _____ Zip _____

RE: Employee _____ *(Print name here)* _____

SS # _____

I, _____ *(Signature of applicant here)* _____ , authorize release of employment information requested herein. The above named person has provided your name as their current or previous employer. Please take a moment to verify the following information.

        Supervisor _____

        Position Held _____

        Dates of Employment _____

        Monthly Earnings $ _____

        Full or Part Time_____

        Employment Permanent or Temporary _____

        Reason for Leaving_____

        Comments _____

        _____

        _____

        _____

We request that you verify this information within three working days. Your input is crucial to our rental application process. If you anticipate any delays, we respectfully request that you phone the information to our office. The phone number is listed above.

Sincerely,

_____

Signature of Landlord

      (Company Name) _____

      (Rental Address) _____

      (City, State, Zip) _____

Summary of Move In Fees

for

(Company Name) _____

(Rental Address) _____

(City, State, Zip) _____

Non refundable	$ _____	Application fee
	$ _____	Cleaning fee
	$ _____	First Month's rent
Refundable*	$ _____	Key Deposit
	$ _____	Security Deposit
	$ _____	**Total**

These fees must be paid prior to moving into the unit. All subsequent rental payments are due on or before the first of each month.

Personal checks will not be accepted for the move in fees. Funds may be paid in cash, USPO money order or by certified check from any local bank.

*The Security Deposit is refundable minus any fees for damage, unpaid rent or unpaid utility bills. Key deposit will be refunded when all keys are returned. Please note that security deposits are placed in an interest bearing account. If you leave my property undamaged I will refund your security deposit *plus* the interest it has earned.

Date _____

Hazard Letter

(Company Name)   _____
(Rental Address)   _____
(City, State, Zip)   _____

Tenant's Name   _____
Street   _____
City, State, Zip   _____

Dear _____ :

    I want to make the place where you live as safe as it can be. I am constantly on the lookout for anything around your rental unit which might prove hazardous to life, limb or property. But hard as I try, I cannot uncover every potential danger. I need your help and cooperation.

    Because you are around the property much more than I, you have a greater opportunity to notice hazards. Please report to me, in writing, anything you notice which you think might prove hazardous to you or anyone else. I will investigate and remedy as necessary.

    Please complete the bottom section of the letter and return it to me with your next rent payment. Thank you for your cooperation.

Sincerely,

_____
Signature of Landlord

••

_____ I know of nothing which appears to be unsafe.

_____ I would like to call your attention to the following unsafe conditions:

_____
Signed   Date

Date _____

Insurance Notice

(Company Name) _____
(Rental Address) _____
(City, State, Zip) _____

Tenant's Name _____
Street _____
City, State, Zip _____

Dear _____ :

Each year I review my insurance policies and the coverage of your rental unit. My policy covers only the building itself. It does not cover your belongings.

It is your responsibility to provide insurance to protect yourself in the event of damage, negligence or theft. To protect yourself against any calamity I suggest that you purchase a renters policy.

Your lease requires that you periodically check your smoke detectors for proper operation. Please perform an inspection today.

Sincerely,

_____
Signature of Landlord

Date _____

Notice of Intention to Enter

    (Company Name)   _____
    (Rental Address)   _____
    (City, State, Zip)   _____

    Tenant's Name   _____
    Street   _____
    City, State, Zip   _____

Dear _____ :

    You are hereby notified that at or about _____ am or pm, on _____ 19____, the owner, manager, owner's agent or owner's employees intend to enter your unit.

    The purpose for entry is:
_____
_____
_____

    You are not required to wait for us or remain at home. If the locks have been changed, a locksmith will be called to open the door and rekey the lock. This will be charged to you and must be paid with the next rental payment.

    This is intended to be reasonable notice. If you have a valid reason for asking us to not enter your unit, you must give such request in writing to the manager six hours prior to the date and time specified above for entry.

    This notice was personally delivered by _____.

_____   _____
Date and time delivered   Owner/Manager

Rental History Worksheet

Present Residence

Lease Term _____ to _____
Monthly Rent _____
Number of NSF checks _____
Apartment Damage (describe and estimate amount) _____
_____

Notice Given _____
Pets _____
Would you re-rent? ☐ Yes ☐ No
Comments _____
_____

Number of Late Payments _____
Eviction/Skip _____

Outstanding Balance _____
Noise Complaints _____

Immediate Previous Residence

Lease Term _____ to _____
Monthly Rent _____
Number of NSF checks _____
Apartment Damage (describe and estimate amount) _____
_____

Notice Given _____
Pets _____
Would you re-rent? ☐ Yes ☐ No
Comments _____
_____

Number of Late Payments _____
Eviction/Skip _____

Outstanding Balance _____
Noise Complaints _____

Previous Residence of Co-Applicant

Lease Term _____ to _____
Monthly Rent _____
Number of NSF checks _____
Apartment Damage (describe and estimate amount) _____
_____

Notice Given _____
Pets _____
Would you re-rent? ☐ Yes ☐ No
Comments _____
_____

Number of Late Payments _____
Eviction/Skip _____

Outstanding Balance _____
Noise Complaints _____

Verified by _____   Title _____   Date _____

Notes _____
_____
_____
_____

Move In And Move Out Inspection Form

Property address and Unit # _____

Resident's Name _____ Phone _____

NOTICE TO RESIDENT: Georgia Law Requires that you acknowledge the correctness of the Move In and Move Out inspection reports by signing or, if you disagree, by filing a properly signed written statement of dissent setting forth specifically those items with which you disagree.

Location of Damage	**Move In Inspection**	**Move Out Inspection**
Exterior		$_____
Entrance Foyer and Powder Room		$_____
Dining Room		$_____
Kitchen and Eat In Area		$_____
Living Room		$_____
Bedroom and Bath Room Upstairs		$_____
Master Bedroom and Bath		$_____
Other		___ Keys returned ☐ Yes ☐ No Lock Rekeyed $_____
Hallway, Stairs, Washer and Dryer		$_____

Move In Inspection delivered to resident prior to occupancy and prior to acceptance of any security deposit.

Move Out Inspection results delivered to resident

_____
Landlord   **Date**

Resident accepts responsibility for condition of above referenced rental property "as is" with the exceptions noted above. This form is made a part of the rental agreement. Resident acknowledges receipt of Move In Inspection results prior to occupancy and prior to acceptance of any security deposit. Resident has inspected the property prior to occupancy and accepts Move In Inspection report.

_____
Landlord   **Date**

Inspection to determine extent and estimated charges for any damage to be assessed by landlord against resident. Resident acknowledges receipt of Move Out Inspection report and estimated costs.

_____
Resident   **Date**

_____
Resident   **Date**

Notice of Intention To Vacate

(Submit to landlord sixty days prior to moving)

TO: ACME APARTMENTS

FROM: _____

UNIT #: _____

DATE: _____

Please be advised that on _____, 19_____ I/We intend to move from our residence at Acme Apartments, Unit # _____.

I/We hereby give _____ days notice that we do not intend to renew our rental agreement with Acme Apartments.

I/We further understand that rental payments must be paid through the term specified in our lease agreement. Our last rental payment is due on_____, 19_____

I/We understand that you will refund my/our security deposit within 30 days after I/we have moved out. Please send the move out inspection report and security deposit to my/our forwarding address:

_____

_____

TENANT_____

TENANT_____

RECEIVED BY_____

DATE_____

ABOUT THE AUTHOR

Mary Farmer began her landlording career in 1990. She is a graduate of Samford and Auburn Universities. Neither prepared her for landlording. Currently, Farmer is pursuing a BFA from Georgia State University.

Farmer is active in The League of Women Voters, Project Open Hand/ Atlanta and Georgia Citizens for the Arts. This is her first book.

ORDER FORM

Global Interests Press · 690 Greystone Park · Atlanta, GA 30324
phone (404) 892-0100 · fax (404) 872-4591

I would like to order :   ____ copies @ $12.95 each $ _____

Georgia Sales Tax at 6% $ _____

Shipping/Handling @ $3.00/book $ _____

Total Due $ _____

Please send book(s) to:

_____
Name

_____
Street

_____
City   State   Zip Code

_____
Daytime Phone   Date

_____
Visa/Mastercard Number   Expiration Date

_____
Signature (Required if using credit card)

Sorry, we cannot accept personal checks. Send US funds in the form of a cashier's check or money order, or include Visa/Master Card information.

Thanks for your order.